Wild Kat

THE BIOGRAPHY OF JESSIE WALLACE

EMILY HERBERT

Published by John Blake Publishing Ltd,
3, Bramber Court, 2 Bramber Road,
London W14 9PB, England

www.blake.co.uk

First published in hardback in 2006

ISBN 1 84454 223 8

British Library Cataloguing-in-Publication Data:

A catalogue record for this book is available from the British Library.

Design by www.envydesign.co.uk

Printed in Great Britain by Creative Print & Design, Wales

1 3 5 7 9 10 8 6 4 2

Papers used by John Blake Publishing are natural, recyclable products made from
wood grown in sustainable forests. The manufacturing processes conform to the
environmental regulations of the country of origin.

Photographs © Big Pictures p1, p3, p5; Empics p5, p6; Getty Images p1, p4;
Mirrorpix p4; Rex Features p2, p3, p4, p5, p6, p7, p8.

Contents

Kitty Kat

Jessie Wallace is one of the most popular faces on television today. At the beginning of the twenty-first century, she virtually became a star overnight, catapulted from a completely unknown actress with little professional acting experience to one of the best-known faces in the UK, and all because of her character in *EastEnders* called Kat. Her life since then has not always run smoothly.

In some ways as volatile as her on-screen character – although Jessie is always keen to emphasise the differences between herself and Kat – she has become a favourite not only with the public, but also with the tabloids, who are keen to chart the minutiae of every aspect of her life.

So far, it has been quite a life, filled with incident and drama and a rise from humble beginnings to major celebrity. And her career looks set to go further still.

Despite the odd mishap, BBC bosses have made it clear to Jessie that she has a future far beyond her current role in *EastEnders*; a highly talented actress with a natural warmth that has captivated audiences everywhere, she has the potential to end up as one of the profession's greats. But just who is she really? And where does she come from? For, when Jessie first entered the world, no one had a clue they were dealing with a baby and then a child who would one day become a household name.

The time that Jessie was born? The early 1970s. The place? North London – Enfield, to be precise. The event? The birth of Karen Jane Wallace on 25 September 1971, a birthday, incidentally, that she shares with Michael Douglas and Catherine Zeta-Jones. But back then, no one had heard of Michael Douglas, the great Catherine was still in her infancy, and the newcomer just seemed like an ordinary, if much-loved, baby. There was no clue that under the name of Jessie, she would one day become one of the most popular and talked about television stars in Britain.

Indeed, there was nothing in the Wallace family background to signify what the future would hold. Jessie does not come from a theatrical family and her career has taken her nearest and dearest by surprise. She might now be one of the country's most famous names but her talent and ambition had a long way to go before they would be recognised.

Home life was comfortable, although it would not be long before it was to change. Jessie had an older sister, Joanne. Her father, James, was a Telecom engineer; her mother Annette looked after the family; and her grandmother, whom Jessie absolutely adored, lived nearby in Manor House. It is often thought that Jessie is a real East Ender, which is not quite the case, but she does have a link with that area of the capital, as her mother was born there.

But there was upheaval very early on in Jessie's life – something that seems to have caused no lasting damage, but which changed her world as she knew it when she was still a little girl. Jessie's parents divorced when she was three and, unusually, it was her father who cared for the children.

'All I know is that Mum and Dad separated,' Jessie said many years later. 'There wasn't anyone else – she just wasn't happy with my dad. So he looked after me and my big sister Joanne. Dad was brilliant – he was both parents rolled into one. He worked flat out as a Telecom engineer, made sure neither of us ever went without, and was always there for us.'

Indeed, as an adult, Jessie shows none of the emotional insecurity that marks out so many actors and actresses. She was a much-loved little girl, by both her parents and her grandmother. She remains extremely close to her family, something that has never changed as her name became better known. Her father also clearly went to great lengths to make sure she was happy and protected, a strategy that seems to have paid off.

'I don't ever remember coming home from school to an empty house,' she said. 'Whatever hobby I wanted, Dad supported me. He took me to swimming lessons and, when I wanted a guitar, he went out and bought me one – although two weeks later I got bored and gave it up. That's the sort of horrible child I was. I saw Mum at weekends, but I was a real daddy's girl.'

That continues to be the case to this day. Jessie does have women friends but, as she herself says, the majority of her mates are men. Her close and endearing relationship with her father has meant that she feels most comfortable in the company of men.

Both Annette and Jessie were, however, deeply upset by later claims that Annette walked out on the family. 'I'd like to put it right about my mum,' Jessie said. 'Mum never left me when I was three. My parents separated when I was three and I lived with my dad. They've both been there for me and given me 100 per cent support. I love them to bits – both of them.'

Indeed, although she lived with her father, there was never the slightest hint of *froideur* between mother and daughter; the two were always close. It was merely that, unusually, Jessie lived with her father.

Indeed, Jessie's first memories date from the period in

her life when her parents split up. 'I can remember having a bath in the kitchen sink when I was about three years old,' she once said. 'It's a strange thing to remember, but I can see it really vividly. I've got a good memory from when I was young. I even remember my first day at playschool. I recall sitting on the slide and suddenly realising my mum wasn't there. It was then that I burst into tears.'

That early moment of insecurity, however, was not to last – or rather, it was to take on a slightly different form. While she was utterly secure within the family unit, she also had agonising moments of self-doubt, which led her, in turn, to lashing out at anyone around her. Jessie was clearly a handful, as she later admitted. 'I was a horrible child, but never the sadistic type,' she said. 'I wasn't into dynamiting small animals. The first really exciting thing that happened to me was winning a dance contest when I was ten. I had this Buck's Fizz dance that I learnt. I won a beanbag toy that became my pride and joy.'

Her early exuberance frequently led her into scrapes – of which more anon – and is a clear sign of the lively personality she was later to become. For, to put it bluntly, ever since she was a little child to the present day, Jessie has always managed to get into trouble. Whether it's being with the wrong people or ending up at the wrong place at the wrong time, Jessie has always raised eyebrows and that continues even now. But it is also a defining quality that makes her so popular. Because she is not a quiet little mouse who sits in a corner, Jessie does tend to draw attention to herself, whether it's deliberately or not, and that has led her into the odd mess.

Her liveliness did not manifest itself everywhere, however. Although she was an accomplished dancer, Jessie was not a sporty child. 'No, definitely not,' she said, when asked about her sporting prowess. 'I was a good swimmer and used to go quite regularly, but then I became interested in boys and that was it. I also tried synchronised swimming for a week. At school, I was terrible at sport.

'I was always the slowest runner – I used to run like a frog, and my legs used to go in different directions, like a propeller. I was never any good at the high jump, either. I would run up to the pole and then stand there and run back and promise to do it the next time, but I never would. It was too hard. As far as sports and I are concerned, we just don't go together.'

That, again, points up incidents in her life as an adult. Jessie has a voluptuous figure, but there have been occasions when her bosses were concerned it was filling out too much. It wasn't, of course, but Jessie is an actress who is very much in the public eye and so is subject to the same pressures about weight and image that are brought to bear on all actresses. Again, it is an intensely likeable quality that means she doesn't obsess about her appearance in the way some showbusiness figures do, but the industry in which she works has forced her to rethink some aspects of her lifestyle. She may not be sporty, but these days she knows the value of exercise.

Probably the strongest influence in her childhood and, indeed, her life, was the person Jessie always called 'Nan', of whom she saw a great deal because she lived nearby. Jessie adored her grandmother and was extremely close to her – and, indeed, they had the same name. 'I loved Nan to pieces and I was so proud to be named after her,' Jessie said. 'She was my idol, because she was so beautiful and glamorous and such fun. She had the most wonderful jet-black hair, which was natural, unlike mine, and piercing blue eyes. And even if she was just cleaning the house, she'd have lipstick on. She was immaculate.'

Her glamour clearly rubbed off. Jessie has been naturally blessed with a striking appearance, but she heightens it with an acute awareness of what works for her. Latterly, of course, she has been able to indulge herself with the finest designers in the world, but back then she was learning from her grandmother how to put a look together. Their closeness made her all the more willing to learn.

'She lived near us in Manor House, so I saw her quite

a lot,' said Jessie. 'I'd sit and listen as she told me all these stories about life in London during the war. It all sounded so romantic. She's kept lots of her clothes and let me try on all these tailor-made coats and furs. I still love 1940s fashions.

'On Saturday afternoon, I'd sit by her chair and we'd watch old Hollywood films together. She was so loving and always there for me. She used to tell me, "You can be anything you want." It was what I needed to hear.' It was also a fortunate counterbalance to school, where she frequently heard exactly the opposite. Jessie Wallace was not an academic child.

Jessie's grandmother died of cancer at the age of 72 in 1994, years before her granddaughter was to become a household name. '*EastEnders* is the best thing that's ever happened to me, or is ever likely to,' Jessie said. 'And Nan's death was the worst. She was such a bright spirit. When she was in hospital, dying, this doctor came in. He was gorgeous, and Nan went, "Look at him. Isn't he lovely?" She was like a young girl trapped in an old woman's body. I wish she'd lived to see me get this part – she'd have been so proud.'

Back in the days of her childhood, though, Nan was there to offer comfort and reassurance when problems occurred, as well as enthusiasm and encouragement for the future. It was, at times, much needed. Jessie's first school was Ambrose Fleming, where she became known for the kind of disruptive behaviour that was to characterise her later years at school.

'I have fond memories of Jessie,' said a fellow pupil from the time. 'I remember her and me got into trouble because we were fighting other girls in the teachers' car park.' The teachers, of course, were not so impressed.

At her next school, Kingsmead, in Enfield, Middlesex, Jessie certainly made her mark – but unfortunately, again she stood out for all the wrong reasons. There was a good deal of childish behaviour – cheeking the teacher, mild trouble-making and a complete lack of interest in anything to do with the academic side of school life. Jessie herself puts it down to an inner insecurity, which she tried to mask with brashness.

'There was a lot of attention seeking,' she said. 'I was terrible at school. I had no confidence whatsoever and never tried because I just thought I'd fail. I was really horrible. I hated the whole world. If anyone asked me anything, I'd simply snarl back, "You what?" I left at 15 without a single qualification.'

In truth, it was not unusual behaviour for a troubled adolescent, but it certainly meant that no one could forecast back then just how famous the troublesome young Jessie was going to turn out to be.

And Jessie really was troublesome. She frequently landed herself in hot water. 'She was always mucking about,' said one of her contemporaries from school. 'She used to get in a lot of trouble with the teachers. She wasn't a mean girl, but her high spirits certainly caused problems.' Another schoolmate was less forgiving. 'Karen [as Jessie was known then] was a complete bitch, who made other kids' lives a misery with her gang of tough mates,' Harry Grantham said.

Of course, a great many schoolgirls behave badly, in an attempt to make themselves appear cool; the difference is that they don't end up on a famous soap opera two decades later. Jessie's problem was, in reality, not that she was too confident, but that she wasn't confident enough. The teenage years can be extremely difficult and hers were no different, with the added worry that she had no clue about what she wanted to do in the future. Given that exams were not exactly her forte, and nothing else presented itself as the obvious solution, there was a real concern that she would ultimately just allow her life to drift.

Indeed, that was to happen for a while. Jessie was not one of those fortunate actresses who make their name when they are very young; it was to take her years to decide what she really wanted to do, let alone to get on and doing it. But, like the school days she loathed, it all ultimately turned out to be character-building and stood her in good stead.

That did not, however, make her any easier to deal with while she was still at school. On one occasion,

Jessie's high jinks nearly ended in tragedy. At senior school, smoking in the girls' loos, she was playing with a lighter close to another girl's hair. The girl's hair suddenly went up in flames. Fortunately for all concerned, Jessie and her friend managed to put the fire out.

'It was an accident,' Jessie later explained, 'and no one was hurt. She just had lots of hair lacquer on and I was flicking my lighter, and it went – voom! – and the next minute I was banging her head and it went out. But she didn't realise she was on fire, so when I started banging her head, she just turned around and hit me.' It is clear that, in later life, she has been embarrassed by the incident. Back then, however, she was able to laugh it off.

Academically, Jessie continued to underachieve. That contributed to her dislike of school. She clearly felt she was completely wasting her time and that even her presence was useless, which, in turn, only served to make matters worse. 'I hated school,' she said, years later. 'I was so naughty – I'd talk back to the teachers. I was always on report, I used to come to school with different-coloured hair every day. I think it was just attention-seeking. But I was terrible. I hated the whole world and I had no confidence because I thought I was going to fail.' Her feelings were reciprocated in full by a teacher: 'You're a no-hoper… you won't amount to anything,' she said.

But it was while she was at school that the first

intimations of where her life would eventually end up came about. From early on, Jessie was an enthusiastic participant in school plays, although she had no idea at the time that this would one day become her life. It was an ideal channel, both for her frustrations and her desire to make herself the centre of attention; when she was acting, she was both centre stage, and yet, at the same time, someone other than herself.

'When I was at school, I'd always get the lead role in plays and, when I left, I did short drama courses,' she revealed. Cinderella and Dorothy were just two of the roles she took on. It was the one area of schooling that she really enjoyed and she shone at it. Jessie was a natural-born actress, although in time she was to take acting lessons, too.

Being a professional actress would have seemed inconceivable back then, both to Jessie herself and to her family, who were a very typical English lot, and didn't realise that they had a future star on their hands.

Then again, who can blame them? Jessie took a long time to get to where she wanted to go, but once her star finally did start to rise, it was meteoric. She has, to date, had the kind of luck and career that most actresses can only dream of and so it is of little surprise that no one realised the direction in which she should be pointed.

Difficult periods in childhood sometimes pay off in other ways, too. They give the person concerned a desire to prove themselves, an ambition and a determination that many people simply do not have. There's nothing like going nowhere for a while to point people at a particular destination when they finally realise the direction they want to take. Jessie was marked by the feeling of simply drifting for so long that it finally made her get her act together and work hard to achieve her goals.

The Jessie of then could not have believed that she would turn into the Jessie of now – still landing in hot water, certainly, but also working very hard at her career. And she does work at it. It is said that the best acting is to look as if you are not acting at all. Jessie achieves that, and it's thanks to a great deal of hard work behind the scenes.

Despite being a 'star' at drama within the limited confines of her school, her teachers didn't really appreciate her gifts. 'It wasn't obvious to me she was going to end up in *EastEnders*,' said one of Jessie's teachers, Paul Caistor. 'But she had a very outgoing personality and it was clear that she was a very good actress.'

As so often in her life, it was her parents and grandmother who supported her in her dreams and ambitions, although they still had no clue as to where it would take their talented little girl. 'When I was a kid, I was always the lead in plays,' Jessie said on another occasion. 'My parents were not interested in acting at all, but they supported me. My Nan was a real film buff – I used to sit with her on Saturday afternoons and watch old films. It was then that I became interested in acting.' The influence of her grandmother, above everyone else, was what really gave her the strength to go ahead with her plans.

By her teens, Jessie had taken on other interests, too. She was developing into a woman and had started to have boyfriends, something she found considerably more interesting than academic life. Even when she was younger, she had a striking appearance that drew many into her orbit. Jessie has never had a problem in attracting men. Of course, Jessie being Jessie, this has also led to some problems, not least because she has not always been the most careful girl when it comes to affairs of the heart.

Jessie's troubled side came out in other ways, too. She had some health problems, one of which was when she used to suffer from terrible migraines. 'I started suffering migraines when I was about nine,' she recalled. 'I'd get physically sick and have to lock myself away in a dark room. The doctors did all these tests and eliminated all these things from my diet – cheese, orange juice, coffee, chocolate. But nothing helped. The pain was indescribable. It was like someone digging a needle into my right eye.

'As a child I got them every few days and I'd be crying

out in pain. I missed so much school and the medical room became my second home. They eased off after I visited a faith healer in my teens. She was brilliant. I was going out with a bloke at the time and his mum went to see her every week, so I went along for a laugh. She ran her hands above my head and I could feel her pulling the pain out of me.'

The migraines were, however, to go on for years. It was not until comparatively recently that the problem has finally gone away; Jessie herself says that it was when she finally stopped suffering from stress, a condition that would seem, on the whole, to have been self-imposed. But while she outwardly may have had few signs of stress as a child, due to close relationships with all her family, inwardly she continued to have problems.

Despite the troubles at school, Jessie was always close to her family and that didn't change as she was growing up. The home she shared with her father, sister and, ultimately, stepmother, was an extremely secure one. Jessie never grew up with feelings of being unloved. It is not contradictory to say that she was both secure and insecure; all her external circumstances in her family were completely secure. It was only an inability to believe in herself that caused the insecurities that she felt so keenly as she grew up.

The end of school was approaching and, much as they

loved their feisty daughter, her parents were unable to suggest a path they thought she should now follow. Neither could Nan offer the solution to her future. And so it was that, at the age of fifteen, Jessie left school without a single qualification to her name. 'I didn't even bother going back to get my last report because I hardly ever turned up to school anyway,' she later revealed. 'I was such a little cow. My teachers told me, "You're a no-hoper... you're never going to do anything with your life and you won't amount to anything."'

It was a prediction that was rather far from the mark – even if it took some time for Jessie to get up and run.

But Jessie had no particular plan, and no particular idea what she was going to do. There were no family traditions to follow as such, no – at that time – overwhelming ambitions to be fulfilled and no obvious course for Jessie to take. It is a situation many people have found themselves in and then had problems getting out of. When the moment came, however, Jessie managed to come good. For the next couple of years, though, she was to live a life that was quite as difficult as that of her fictional counterpart, Kat.

2

Kiss and Make Up

The deed was done – at the tender age of fifteen, Jessie had left school and, in theory at least, the world was her oyster. For years she had loathed the restrictive environment of formal education, and so her relief to be out of it was palpable. Her family circumstances had also changed; both parents had remarried, with her father now running The Leather Bottle pub in Ingatestone, Essex, and Jessie now had a younger stepsister, Danielle.

Both parents were happy and Jessie was happy for them too. She was also very close to Danielle. 'Jessie has always looked out for me,' Danielle revealed when she, too, entered the world of showbusiness. 'When I was little, I used to wake up in the middle of the night and go to her room. It would be pitch black and the only sound would be me sucking my dummy. I'd wake her up and she'd always say, "Come on then, in you get.'" It is a rather charming image of a domestic Jessie that was not, at that stage, as much in evidence as the wilder version.

But outside her family, the problems remained. What to do next? She had no qualifications, no specific ambitions, no obvious route to take – in short, she had no idea at all what to do. She might have been free of the world of the classroom, but it was freedom at a price. And so, for the next few years, Jessie simply drifted. She hadn't a clue what to do, and it showed.

Although it would not have seemed so at the time, these years were not entirely wasted. Their very aimlessness fired Jessie with an ambition she had not had before. It took several years for it to sink in, but she was finally forced to realise that if she was to do something with her life, she had to start now. It gave her drive, and energy. And it also made her realise when, still a fair few years from now, she got her chance to work on *EastEnders*, quite how lucky she was. There were undoubtedly moments when television stardom went to her head, but underneath it all, she realised quite how fortunate she had been to go from the situation she found herself in after leaving school to the life of a star.

Jessie's first job was packing kilts in a skirt factory. It didn't make her any happier than school had done. She then worked in a bakery in Wood Green. That wasn't much fun, either. She cleaned toilets. She worked in a Benetton store – for one hour. These days, she says that was the worst job of them all. 'I was standing there folding up jumpers and people kept coming in and unfolding them, so I just walked out!' she said. 'I just wasn't happy, so I left!'

Her image was also going through frequent changes. 'I became a Rockabilly girl,' she said, 'then a Hippy, then a Punk, then a Goth.' She was clearly trying to find herself – whoever this 'self' turned out to be. But it was interesting that she was exploring her choices by changing her appearance – the exact same thing that an actress does for a living. Perhaps even then she had a clue as to how it would all turn out.

But it was not an easy time. Jessie still bears the scars from this period – quite literally. One day, she decided to have her belly button pierced and duly went along to have the work done. However, she only realised at the very last minute that the person who was performing the piercing was in no fit state to do the job.

'Years ago, I wanted my belly button pierced and I decided to go and see this dodgy geezer who did piercings and tattoos at home,' she said in 2001. 'Just as he was shoving the skewer into my belly button, I realised he was drunk and then he fell to one side. It went in crooked, so the hole is massive and all lop-sided. The skewer looked like a kebab stick. Maybe it *was* a kebab stick. It was really painful. I wouldn't advise anyone else to do it.'

As if this were not enough, it was also at around this time that Jessie decided to have a tattoo. 'When I was about sixteen, I got this horrible design of pastel-coloured little flowers on my thigh,' she said. 'I've thought about getting it removed, but I might just get another over it.' That is, in fact, just what she went on to do – and the new tattoo reads 'Elvis'. To this day, Elvis is Jessie's hero; she still describes him as her perfect man.

There was one positive to come out of this rather difficult time, however, and that was the formation of a close friendship that endures to this day. 'Her name is Nicky and we have been mates ever since we were about sixteen,' Jessie explained. 'She lives in Enfield and we met when we first started going out socially. She has been my closest buddy ever since. We're true friends and we know all each other's secrets. She found the whole fame thing quite weird at first, but she's used to it now.' In fact, even now Jessie stays close to many people who knew her before she was famous; it has helped her through difficult times and enabled her to keep her feet on the ground.

Workwise, Jessie still had no idea at all what she wanted to do. 'I drifted from one job to another,' she said. 'I worked in endless shops and even had a stall in Greenwich for a while, making my own jewellery.

Then, when I was twenty-one, I went to Portugal for seven months to join some girlfriends. It was the pits. There were seven of us paying £10 a week for a two-bedroom apartment. I had bar jobs but I was always getting sacked.'

In fact, what had initially seemed like an exciting adventure quickly turned into one of the most difficult periods of Jessie's life. With no money, no prospects, and being a long way from home, her situation soon turned out to be desperate. Not only could she not afford the luxuries she has since grown accustomed to, but she could barely afford the necessities either. 'One day, the only way I could afford to eat was by nicking a potato from a shop,' she later recalled. 'I was so scared that I went round this shop for thirty minutes, working up the courage. I was just desperate for a jacket potato.'

Neither did living in an exotic place compensate for the rough side of life. Even in Portugal, £10 a week on an apartment does not go a long way, and her domestic situation was pretty basic. 'It was a horrible, scary time,' Jessie said. 'We lived in a really rough area of the town. I'd walk home late at night from my bar job and all these pimps would be out. I was terrified. I was desperate to get back to England but I didn't have the money.'

But the experience was to prove fortunate in the end. In such circumstances, Jessie had two choices – to sink or to swim. She had got herself into a situation that was difficult to get out of, but she had the sense to realise that if she was to make anything of her life, she had better start now. Like an awful lot of people, she had wasted years; unlike an awful lot of people, however, she had the strength of character needed to make a fresh start for herself while she was still young enough to have a great deal of choice ahead. And so, summoning up all her reserves of strength, Jessie decided to swim.

'Jessie had no qualifications and no prospects – but she's always been able to live on her wits and she has always been a natural actress,' said a friend. 'So she took drastic action.'

The first step was to get back to England; at the end of her tether, Jessie borrowed her fare home. Then came the hard part – deciding what she was actually going to do. In the end, the choice was both straightforward and sensible: Jessie decided to train as a make-up artist, and managed to obtain a place at the College of East London in Tottenham to study Theatrical and Media Make-up, a two-year course. She had, at long last, found something that she really wanted to do.

Not that obtaining a place was easy. Jessie had no qualifications and had to be less than straightforward in her application, something she admitted years later when this period was all well in the past. 'I don't know if I should say this,' she said, 'but I lied about my qualifications. It was the only way I could get in. I'd always been quite artistic and interested in make-up. When I was ten, I got a horror make-up kit because I loved all that blood and gore.'

And so the course began. It was the first time in her life that Jessie had ever really worked hard at anything, but she realised it was make or break. And it paid off, too. At the end of the two – year course, Jessie managed to get a job with the Royal Shakespeare Company as wig assistant and make-up artist, a role she put to good use when her then boyfriend upset her. 'I was seeing a real idiot when I worked as a make-up artist,' she said. 'I got these hairs from a wig I'd been making and put them in his pants. He was itching like mad.'

Another incident happened when she worked with Joseph Fiennes, one of the very first jobs she had. 'It was almost my last job, too,' said Jessie. 'I was curling his hair and, as he looked at me in the mirror, I felt my knees go weak. He is just so gorgeous. Then my hands broke out in a sweat and I dropped these red-hot tongs in his lap. Mercifully, he laughed it off, but it could have been really nasty.'

This was not the only time she had trouble. 'The bigger the name, the more nervous I was,' she revealed. On the last performance of *Martin Guerre*, I put Iain Glen's wig on too far back. He looked permanently surprised throughout the show. I was also an occasional wig-maker and hated it. I was making a wig for someone who shall remain nameless. My dog Bailey was sitting loyally by my side when I trod on his tail and accidentally pulled out chunks of his beautiful hair. I looked at the wig and at my dog... so for several weeks a part of Bailey was on the stage every night!'

More to the point, however, it was as she watched the actors going out on stage that she realised that here was something she wanted to do with her life, too. 'When I was at the Royal Shakespeare Company, I would watch from the wings and think, "I can do that..." So I bit the bullet and started training.' The person who was to help Jessie in her next step was, actually, Iain Glen.

It was he who advised Jessie to apply for drama school, starting with the grandest of the lot – the Royal Academy of Dramatic Art, better known as RADA. 'I got a recall from RADA and I was so excited, but I didn't get in,' she said. Eventually, she was to end up at The Poor School, a drama school set up so that students can go to classes in the evenings, while holding down jobs during the day. It is partly funded by, among others, Joanna Lumley and Sir Cameron Mackintosh. 'Iain was a real star,' said Jessie. 'He was lovely to me. He told me to just go for it. He used to go through my audition pieces with me until I was word perfect, so I owe him a lot.

'It was only later that I realised there were places for kids who wanted to act but didn't have a lot of money, like Anna Scher. That's where lots of *EastEnders* actors went, such as Susan Tully. It would have been great for me to get into acting early but I guess having to struggle a bit makes me who I am.'

Just as she had done when studying to become a make-up artist, Jessie worked hard. But behind the scenes there was turmoil in her life. Years later, after she had become famous in *EastEnders*, she revealed that it was at this time that she became involved in an abusive relationship. Her boyfriend, whom she has never identified, was an actor a couple of years younger than her and, to begin with, she had no idea about his violent side.

'I liked him quite a lot at first and everything seemed to be going fine,' she said. 'Then, when we had our first little disagreement like boyfriends and girlfriends do, he just went berserk and punched me. He blacked my eye and split my lip. Then he just burst into tears and started saying how sorry he was, begging for forgiveness. He hadn't been drinking or anything. I didn't know he was doing steroids until someone told me after we finished. I just couldn't understand why he'd flown off the handle. He was normally so nice.'

This was, alas, just the beginning. Believing her

boyfriend's assurances that this would not happen again, Jessie decided to continue the relationship. Unfortunately, the situation rapidly deteriorated and it was not long before she was attacked again. 'He bust my lip again, then burst into tears,' she said. 'That's when he'd say, "Look what you made me do," and I'd feel sorry for him again. That's how the first few attacks happened.'

The actor didn't confine himself to Jessie, either; she believes he even went after her dog, too. 'I came home from drama school and found my little shih-tzu Bailey unconscious,' she said. 'It was as if he'd been hit round the head. After that, the dog would wee himself every time he came near. Maybe he attacked Bailey because he was my little dog and I loved and mollycoddled him. Perhaps he was jealous – I don't know. He was very, very sick. At the time, I thought, "No, he wouldn't do that." I couldn't believe anyone would do that to a dog. Maybe he just liked to be powerful.'

Despite the violence, Jessie stayed with him, but it was when she discovered that he'd been seeing someone else that she finally decided she'd had enough. The ensuing attack, however, was the most serious yet. 'I found out he was seeing someone behind my back and I went round to his place with two friends and caught him with the girl,' Jessie said. 'I lost my temper with him. He smacked me round the face and I went flying. He had a corridor in his home with wooden flooring and he sent me flying down it and closed the door behind him so no one could see what he was doing. He picked me up and tried to strangle me. He punched me so hard on the jaw I thought I'd broken my neck.

'Then he sat on me and started banging my head on the floor. I was screaming, "Why are you doing this?" And he said, "Because you're hitting me." It was like he was trying to make it sound like it was the other way around and I was attacking him because the door was shut and my friends couldn't see. I eventually got out of the house. I had a cab waiting outside. I was in the back of the car and couldn't get my head off the seat. I just couldn't stop crying.'

Horrifying as the attack was, it finally made Jessie realise that the relationship was doomed. Indeed, so bad had it been that she actually had to go to hospital, where she was treated for a dislocated jaw. 'I thought he was going to kill me,' she said. 'My jaw still clicks where he dislocated it with a punch. After half-a-dozen beatings, that was it. My little niece was in hospital with meningitis and I couldn't go and see her because of my face. I didn't want my family to see what he'd done to me but, in the end, they had to. They couldn't believe the state of my face. My mum is my witness, my family are my witnesses, and my friends... they saw my face black-and-blue.'

Indeed, Jessie's mother Annette was deeply shocked when she discovered what had been happening to her daughter. 'When your children get hurt, as a parent, it hurts you as well,' she said. 'When he was with her, I know he hit her a few times. I only found out a few weeks afterwards... as she found the whole thing so traumatic, she didn't like to talk about it.

'I saw the injuries when he hit her in the face and hurt her jaw. Her lip was very swollen. I didn't see them when he smashed her head, because those kind of head injuries aren't so visible, but she told me all about it later. I met him a couple of times. He seemed nice at first but, of course, I didn't know what was going on. I think he had very bad mood swings. It was only later that the awful truth came out.'

Jessie has never named him, and revealed that it was only because of pressure from his family that she ended up talking about the incident at all. It clearly brought back difficult memories, but she was respected for it and eventually came to be pleased that she had talked publicly about what happened to her. 'I didn't want to do it – it's something that I'd rather forget,' she said. 'But this ex-boyfriend thought he could sell a story about me, and I didn't think it was fair, considering what he'd put me through, so I had no choice but to do it, to stop him. I'm glad now, though, because a lot of women wrote to me afterwards saying it helped them. So that made it all worthwhile.'

Coping with a violent lover wasn't the only turmoil that Jessie faced. Years later, when she had become a star, she was intensely embarrassed by the revelation that she had had an early conviction involving drink driving. In 1998, she was arrested on Wanstead High Street in North London, in a red Ford Fiesta, and charged with driving under the influence of alcohol.

An enraged Jessie refused to take a Breathalyser test, and when the case came to court in November 1998, the drink-driving charge was dropped. Nonetheless, she was convicted of failing to take the test, banned from driving for fifteen months and ordered to pay £145. It was the first of two such incidents, and the second was to have much wider implications for her life.

As if that wasn't enough, it was at this time that she finally decided to have a breast reduction. Jessie is short, only five-foot one, and so felt that her generous chest was beginning to make her seem as if there was too much on top. She went from an E-cup to a C-cup. 'At five-foot one, I was top heavy and unhappy with my appearance,' she said. 'It took a lot of courage, but it was a success and gave me a lot more confidence.' On another occasion, she was less forthcoming. 'It was a long time ago and it was for personal reasons,' she said, after she had become famous for appearing in *EastEnders*. 'I'm very happy with them now, my little puppies!'

Despite all the trauma in her personal life, however, Jessie continued to study to become an actress, the career she was now certain she wanted to follow. She graduated from The Poor School in 1999 but, to begin with, had little success in finding a role that suited her and took a bar job at her local, The Royal Oak, in Loughton, Essex, to keep her going while she looked for acting work. She was a popular member of staff. 'She was with us for about a year-and-a-half,' said Karen Woodroof, who used to be the landlady of the pub.

'She was very funny and used to make the customers laugh. She never lost her temper like Kat does in the show. And she didn't dress as tarty as she does in *EastEnders*. I am so proud of her.' One of the regulars also remembers her with appreciation. 'She looked exactly as she does in *EastEnders*,' he said. 'She wore really tight gear and all the lads in the pub really fancied her.'

A series of ambitions began, in which Jessie put herself up for just about anything, not least the chorus of the West End musical, *Sunset Boulevard*. 'There were all these skinny birds with legs up to their armpits, with the dance tights and leotards on and short little me,' she later recalled. 'At that time, I had bright red hair and I remember the director hissing to someone, "Get that red-haired girl off my stage!"'

Her aspirations were quite different. After *EastEnders* began, she was asked what her dream acting role would be and replied, 'To play a part like Miranda Richardson did in *Dance with a Stranger*. I'd love to do a really powerful female role. I would like to do theatre work as well – I think it must be a buzz to perform in front of a live audience every night. I enjoyed the atmosphere of theatre in drama school.'

Life was not easy at that time. Jessie had no money at all and, at times, lived as basic a life as she had done in Portugal. 'I lived on stuffing on toast, but there were times I couldn't even afford the loaf of bread. It was hard,' she said.

A break, of sorts, came about when Jessie appeared on television for the first time in *The Bill*. The role was a short one, but it did get her on to the small screen, an achievement that she did not take lightly. 'I played a policewoman and had the uniform, the whole bit,' she said. 'I was so nervous but when I watched myself, I couldn't believe I'd done it.'

She was also doing the odd stage role, with one moment that was so embarrassing it could have put her off her new profession for life. 'I was playing the part of Nell Gwynn in a show called *Playhouse Creatures*,' she later confessed. 'For one scene, I had to pull a sixpence out of my basque. But as I reached inside to extract the coin, my boob fell out.

'The whole place suddenly seemed to go deathly silent. And I knew that the incident could make or break me. So I had to act quickly. So I just pushed my breast back in and continued. It worked. I did get a few cheeky remarks after the show, however. But I thought the whole scenario was hilarious. I managed to save myself from being too embarrassed by making it appear as if it were part of the drama.'

Her big break came soon afterwards. Jessie had auditioned for *EastEnders* in a walk-on role as a party guest; she had made an impression on the show's producers, and was invited back for a week-long workshop. 'It was a big workshop, with fifty or sixty actors,' she later recalled. 'They didn't know what they were looking for, so they just put us all together to see what happened. After two or three days, I had an idea they were looking for a family because there were all these dark-haired girls at the auditions. They picked the actors first, then wrote the characters around us.'

But four months were to pass until she learned that she was to get the part. Jessie was so shocked she passed out in the street. 'I was walking home along Loughton High Street when my agent rang and told me I'd got the part,' she said. 'The next thing I knew, my face was wet. It was really weird. It was like I'd had a blackout in the street. And then I realised that people were staring at me because I was in floods of tears. I was so excited, my agent had to walk me home over the phone. He kept saying, "Keep calm. You're nearly there. Now put your key in the door. Walk inside."' It was a dream come true – Karen Wallace, now known to all as Jessie, was to be a television star at last.

3

The Square
Gets Slatered

The month was September 2000. A new family
were about to move into the most famous
fictional square in Britain, Albert Square, the very heart
of *EastEnders*, and they were set to become one of the
most talked – about set of characters the soap had seen
so far. They were the Slaters and their arrival was one
of the most keenly anticipated in the history of
EastEnders to date. Indeed, so well established have they
become that it is sometimes easy to forget what
relatively recent arrivals they have been. They made
their mark almost upon the moment of their arrival.

There was a buzz about them right from the start. It's
always risky to introduce new characters into a well-
established, much-loved soap but, in this case, the

producers of the show were going one step further because of the sheer volume of them. This was not just one new addition to the cast, nor even two, but a large number of new actors and actresses, who had to be amalgamated into the proceedings as smoothly as possible, both making their presence felt and yet, at the same time, not upsetting the status quo.

It was a huge undertaking, made all the more difficult by the fact that the eyes of the nation were upon them. Even before they appeared, an enormous amount of publicity had been generated by the new arrivals, which meant that there was both an enormous expectation for them to live up to and an even more enormous amount for them to lose if they all fell flat on their faces. In the event, of course, as the world now knows, the whole undertaking proved to be the most enormous success.

And Jessie was part of the new gang. She was to play Kat Slater, later Moon, the tart with a heart and a barmaid at the Queen Vic. There were vast numbers of other Slaters – Zoë, who was introduced as her sister but turned out to be something else; Charlie, her father; Mo, her grandmother; Belinda, Little Mo and Lynne, her sisters; Harry, her uncle; and others too numerous to mention. There were quite a few love interests, too. And so, on 18 September 2000, Jessie Wallace made her first appearance in the most famous fictional location of East London of all time.

Jessie herself, needless to say, was absolutely thrilled. This is the kind of break that every actor and actress waits for and very few actually get. And for it to happen so soon after she had entered her new profession was particularly amazing. She might have paid her dues in terms of getting nowhere in her late teens and early twenties, but she was about to make up for all that lost time in a very big way. She had, as yet, however, no real idea of what would await her. At the time she was a complete unknown — about to step, almost overnight, into great fame. And as she was to discover, nothing can prepare even the most savvy for what happens next.

And so Jessie set about making the part her own, in her own inimitable way. In her earliest interviews, she announced that she would be basing the character of Kat on the girls near where she then lived in Loughton, Essex, going on to call them 'lazy tarts'. The ladies of Loughton were less than thrilled by this accolade, and responded that it takes one to know one. But it was all taken in good part and, of course, the publicity did nothing to harm the growing amount of interest in the Square's new arrivals. And it was an interest that was to rocket as the months went by. It was also an early indication that Jessie tended to make the headlines almost every time she opened her mouth. A star was very much in the making.

There was, however, said to be jealousy in some quarters surrounding the show and it would have been surprising if that hadn't been the case. The producers were determined to get their new characters to start off with a bang, with the result that the feeling in some quarters was that they were getting the best storylines, and not everyone was thrilled about that. And then there were also the viewers to think about. They were used to *EastEnders* in the format that it then was and to bring in so many new characters and allow them to dominate the storyline risked changing the face of the programme altogether. In the event, of course, it was a gamble that paid off.

But the early days were not all plain sailing. A couple of years later, Jessie was asked if people had been welcoming when she joined the show. 'I think because we came as a group of people, the Slaters, this big, loud family, we took some getting used to – the audience didn't like us at first,' she said. 'It took them a while to warm to us.'

That was as maybe. Kat herself was an enormously popular character right from the start and, if truth be told, there were some people who thought that the role had been based on Jessie herself, then she took it with a pinch of salt. 'Well, I suppose they must have seen a bit of Kat in me,' she said. 'I'm not as brash as Kat, but I can be like her. The good thing is that she's got so many sides. She's tough on the outside but so much bad stuff has happened to her that you can understand her attitude.'

In later years, it turned out that the story about Kat being based on Jessie had more truth to it than anyone realised at the time. Tony Jordan, who worked as a consultant on *EastEnders*, said that Kat was created the moment Jessie walked into the room where the new boys and girls were doing a workshop. 'I don't know how to take that!' said Jessie. 'It's hard to say how much is me, because Kat's changed so much since the early episodes. She seemed a bit mixed up then, and I didn't really know how she was going to turn out. I remember smiling for photographers during our first publicity session, thinking, "I don't know who this character is, or what she's going to be like." So I don't know what Tony Jordan saw, but it must have been something!'

It was indeed. And back then, there was something almost childishly pleasing about the way Jessie was reacting to what had happened. There was a kind of joyousness about her, for she was well aware her life would change in her new role, although the extent of it was to take her by surprise. She was stunned by her good luck and almost disbelieving that it had happened. And she wanted others to share in her good fortune.

In a manner that was typical both of Jessie and the character she was going to play, she immediately went shopping. 'I promised my best mate Stuart, a singer and dancer I met when I was doing make-up, and his boyfriend Keith that I'd buy them something from my first wage packet,' she revealed. 'While I was there, I couldn't resist getting myself something, too.' Indeed, she began to splash out on clothes and jewellery in a way she previously couldn't have dreamt of doing. A car was on the shopping list, too, a midnight-blue Golf.

Her extended family were thrilled for her, and there were quite a few of them, now. Joanne had by this time married Mo – not to be confused with Little Mo, who was both fictional and a woman – and the two of them lived in Romford, Essex, with their five children. The sisters remained close and Joanne was delighted that life for her little sister was turning out so well. Her parents were utterly thrilled, too. Their little Jessie, the sometimes difficult child who had seemed, at times, to have no idea what to do with her life, was going to be famous. That was not a hope – it was a given. Anyone who spent any time in the Queen Vic was certain to become a talking point in the real-life bars and pubs across the land.

Jessie was quite awestruck the first time she visited the fictional Albert Square itself, and it soon became a favourite place to loiter between takes. 'The first time I visited Albert Square was when I found out I'd got the part,' she said. 'I was taken round on a tour and I came out on the Square and I just had a fit of the giggles.' This was hardly surprising. Albert Square has become almost as famous as any real London location, and many people who see it for the first time feel that it is uncannily familiar. And Jessie was not just any old visitor; she was actually going to spend her working life in the place.

But like so many before her, she discovered that fantasy and reality are not always the same thing. Acting is based on illusion, and that applied to the location as much as anything else. Albert Square in real life is quite different from Albert Square in *EastEnders*, something that many first-time viewers take a moment to adjust to. But Jessie soon made it a place she liked to hang out in when other people weren't around.

'It was really surreal,' said Jessie. 'The first time I walked on to the Square, I couldn't believe how tiny it was. It's not quiet that often, but it's great when we're not filming on the lot. There's a residential area right close by the square, too, but you still never hear anything. I used to pinch myself. The first time it hit me was when I was doing a scene hanging out of my bedroom window. Kat's first boyfriend turned up and her nan threw a bucket of water over him. In between shots, all the Vic was lit up and I was looking over at it and I just wanted to cry because I thought, "I work here… I work in Albert Square." And it's brilliant.'

That was putting it mildly. There has been much debate about *EastEnders* of late, as to whether it's been too depressing, or whether its storylines are quite right or what its characters have been getting up to off screen, but the fact of the matter is that twenty years after its inception, it remains one of the most popular soaps that has ever been broadcast on British television. It was the stuff of dreams for an actor to get a part on it and it was the beginning of a series of doorways that were to open to Jessie that she had previously never even known existed. It was the chance of a lifetime.

And no matter how much Jessie thought she might have been prepared for what was going to happen to her, nothing is ever quite as people think it will be, and Jessie was staggered when people started recognising her in the street. Remember, unlike many actors and actresses, she had not built up a public profile slowly, and garnered the attention that went with it on an escalating scale, but went from nought to a hundred – in terms of recognition – overnight.

One day, she was just another women on the street, albeit it a very attractive one; the next, she was very nearly public property. And Jessie had to get used to the fact that from now on, people were going to stop and stare. 'The first time it happened, I wondered if I'd walked out naked,' she said. 'I couldn't understand why everyone was laughing at me. Now I know it's just nerves. I seem to be a hit with little girls – they love Kat because she's fun and outspoken.'

Indeed, Kat almost immediately became something of a sensation. Boys fancied her, girls empathised with her and, of course, there was increasing interest in the actress who played her. There was a gutsiness to both Kat and Jessie that was immensely appealing. They both exuded warmth and both had a bit of a temper. Jessie kept emphasising that she was very different from Kat, but the popularity of the latter translated into great affection for the former. In no time at all, Jessie had become one of the nation's favourite actresses. It was exhilarating stuff.

And she didn't just become famous; Kat/Jessie even became something of a role model, although Jessie was sensible enough to realise that when fans started to emulate her, it was Kat they were looking up to, not Jessie. That came later, when she became more of a known quantity in herself.

'[Little girls] think everything about Kat is good,' Jessie revealed. 'Most of them love her look the best, the way she dresses, her attitude – the lot. They just love Kat. There is always a bulging bag of mail waiting for me when I get home from work. I get a lot of letters and they are always full of questions. They always want to know where I get my handbags, where the frocks are from, the shoes, whatever. I reply to the letters and tell them where to buy it. If they take the time to write, I'll always reply to them.'

They loved Kat's character, but then, as time went on, they loved Jessie, too. She was one of them, with the same tastes they had, the same heroes and heroines and, in many ways, the same aspirations. Jessie and her fans came from the same background, which meant that when she talked about her life, they could relate to much of that, too. Some actors and actresses appear to come from a different planet; Jessie looked as if she came from just down the road and she had no airs and graces, no side to her. And, just like her fans, she was capable of looking up to showbusiness personalities, too.

For example, when asked about her heroine, she cited someone who is not only adored the planet over, but who has, for decades, struck a chord with teenage girls. 'I think Madonna is brilliant and she just keeps on getting better and better,' Jessie said. 'When she first started out with the lace gloves and everything, I was about twelve and I tried to dress up like her. I wore ribbons in my hair and had leg-warmers. I still love her music.'

And this also led another group of women to empathise with Jessie. When Madonna started out, she famously inspired hordes of young teenage girls to become 'wannabes', who dressed and tried to act like their heroine. These girls had now grown up and were about Jessie's age – and delighted to discover that she had been a wannabe, too.

Her hero struck even more of a common touch. Asked about her ideal man, she replied, 'Elvis Presley in every way! I've even got pictures of him on my wall that I can look at whenever I want to! I like the actor Michael Madsen as well because he looks a bit like Elvis! I even recorded the film *Free Willy* off the TV recently just because he's in it.' A girl who loved Elvis and Madonna? No wonder Jessie had so much in common with her fans.

But much as she loved her new life, Jessie didn't want to be confused with the character she played. For example, she was always adamant that she and Kat had nothing in common when it came to clothes. 'I don't dress like Kat – I wouldn't be seen dead in her foul leather jacket and I detest red,' she said. "I like autumn colours.'

Indeed, it soon became clear that quite apart from the fact that she now had money to spend, Jessie had an enormous amount of style. New ensembles began to appear which were, indeed, a good deal more tasteful than those Kat ever put on, and which frequently graced the front covers of magazines. Jessie's wardrobe was expanding quite a bit; gone was the experimenting with styles like Punk and Goth, and in came more elegant outfits from the fashion mainstream.

Any woman who likes clothes would have been thrilled to find herself in Jessie's position; as she said herself, she had gone from being so poor that she had to eat stuffing on bread, to being able to splash out on designer clothes. It was certainly not the main reason she'd wanted to be in *EastEnders*, but it was an added benefit, all the same.

But the differences between Jessie and the character she played remained. Jessie maintained that Kat was far more of a man-eater than she was, something she commented on when Kat went after dishy Doctor Anthony, another new resident in the Square. 'I could never do that,' she said. 'I'm far too shy – I've never asked a man out in my life.' Men were certainly interested in her, however – Jessie was delighted when she realised that she was beginning to be seen as a real sex symbol, although she also sometimes confessed to feeling a little bemused.

But she did express great sympathy for the character she played, stating that if they met in real life, she was sure they would get on. 'You could really let yourself go with Kat and not worry about anything because she would just go mad!' said Jessie. 'She's the sort of girl you could dare to do anything and she would do it. We're quite similar in some ways.

'I've actually been noticing it more and more recently – I'm not sure if she's turning into me, or I'm turning into her! Kat would definitely be the louder one if we went on a night out together. Our main similarity is that we're both very loyal to our friends and the members of our family. I'm very glad I don't dress like her, though!'

Jessie was also fully supportive of her character. Asked what she would like to change about Kat, Jessie replied, 'Absolutely nothing. I think Kat Slater is great the way she is. I love the fact she is so upfront with everybody and says exactly what she thinks all the time. If Kat wants something, she will just go out and get it, and she really doesn't care what anyone thinks about her or her appearance. I really love Kat... she's just right the way she is!'

Something else quite extraordinary happened, too. Jessie stopped suffering from the migraines that had plagued her ever since she was a child. 'When I was waiting to hear from *EastEnders*, the headaches got really bad and I started suffering from insomnia, too,' she said shortly after she took on the role. 'I was a wreck. Now they've just gone – I'm convinced that it must be because I'm no longer under stress. My life is just brilliant at the moment.'

Of course, now that she was an actress proper, she was also beginning to bump into other actors she'd known in her make-up artist days. One of these, Nigel Harman, who plays Dirty Den's son Dennis Rickman, and whose character seduced Kat shortly after turning up in Albert Square, had first met her when he was in a West End musical. 'I get on well with Jessie Wallace and we know each other from *Mamma Mia!*,' he revealed. 'We worked there together when she was a make-up artist.' Now, of course, she was on the receiving end of the eyebrow pencil.

Not that Jessie missed her old life. Asked if she hankered after it, she replied, 'No, not really because I'm so happy with what I am doing now. It was weird when people first started doing my make-up here but now I've got used to being pampered, actually. My mates still try and get me to do their make-up when we go on big nights out, but I generally try and get out of it.' But it was a good way of keeping her feet on the ground and remembering that, not long before, her life had been very different indeed.

It was not all sweetness and light, though. Stardom brought with it all sorts of pressures that Jessie had not had to deal with before. While she had always been concerned about her appearance, this was the first time it had become an element in her working life. Newspapers and magazines had started to comment on how she looked and while, on the whole, these comments were complimentary, the pressure was on to look good. And it was not always easy. The camera does not only add ten pounds… it exposes fat where previously there had been none, fills out even the sveltest of figures and provides a very harsh filter through which to be seen.

This was not in itself a problem. Jessie is both striking and photogenic, and there were certainly no issues about giving her a make-over before she was ready to be put in the public eye. But it did mean she was going to have to think seriously about diet and fitness regimes, something that had never been a big issue for her before.

'At drama school, we used to do T'ai Chi and lots of dance and movement exercise,' she said. 'It really helped me tone up, and I lost loads of weight and became really flexible. But, as soon as I left, I went really downhill again, and I've never had the push to do it since. I much prefer mind/body exercise because cardiovascular exercise is just so boring, unless it's dancing, which I love.

'I go out dancing every weekend. It's such a great feeling to dance so much that the next day your bum's killing you. I go to different places all the time because I like dancing to all sorts of music, from '30s and '40s jazz to modern-day music. I like everything, apart from heavy dance music – I find it gets monotonous after a while.'

Jessie was clearly in two minds about the amount of exercise she had to take. 'I don't work out, so I suppose

I'm more of a vegger,' she said. 'I have stages of doing exercise for about two weeks, and then I get bored. I joined a gym a while ago and did lots of cardiovascular exercises, but then I found I got completely obsessed with it. I would spend two hours in the gym, and then come out and scoff my face with chocolate. To veg out, I like reading and spending time with my mates – I think that's really important.'

But this rather reluctant approach to maintaining her figure had its benefits, too. It helped to keep Jessie very much as the 'girl next door'; every woman could sympathise with her feelings about exercise and keeping trim. In fact, there have not been many occasions when the country took to a new soap star as rapidly as they did to Jessie. There was nothing at all of the Hollywood diva about her; she was just a young woman straining, like everyone else, to look good.

'I don't eat much chocolate, which is quite rare for most girls, I think,' she said. 'I have quite a normal diet and I'm not obsessed with what I eat. I like the occasional burger, and have a tendency to eat bad fatty foods that make me feel guilty, but life is too short, really. I have started to watch my weight a bit, more since I started on *EastEnders*, but it fluctuates a lot, anyway, depending on the phase I'm going through, so it's not easy to control. It depends on the time of year as well, and how many parties I've got to go to.'

In fact, in an industry obsessed with appearance, Jessie came over as being remarkably normal. The young girls who constituted so much of her fan base could relate entirely to what she was saying, while men clearly enjoyed the company of a woman who looked nice while making practically no fuss. In fact, in this case, Jessie was an exemplary role model – she simply lived as most normal people do, within the confines of being an actress. She was also extremely self-deprecatory, as well.

'Because I'm only five foot one inch, I can't afford to put on a lot of weight or I end up looking like an Oompa Loompa from *Charlie and the Chocolate Factory*,' Jessie said. 'If I were tall then it wouldn't bother me, but being quite short, I have to be a bit careful. Sometimes, I see myself on wide screen, which makes me look wide, and that makes me think I must cut back.

'It's nice to be a normal size, and I do feel comfortable about my body most of the time, but every now and again, I pull my socks up. I never go on diets, though – I just eat three meals a day and try not to pig out. As long as you discipline yourself, you should be all right.' It is an attitude that has served her well. Jessie has never gone to either extreme when it comes to food – too much or too little – and has managed to look the part without becoming obsessed.

In no time at all, she was featuring even more on the

front covers of magazines, doing interviews and answering questions about her life. And Jessie was not, at the beginning, putting a foot wrong. She was fulsome in her praise for her new show and, indeed, some of its most famous characters. Asked what soap character she would have played if she could, she replied, 'It would have to be Angie Watts because I think she was just brilliant. She was one of the greatest soap females ever. She was in *EastEnders* during my favourite era as well. She was very funny, always glamorous and was a typical East End landlady. I would have loved to have played that character.' It was a very tactful reply and went down extremely well.

It wasn't just past glories that were singled out for praise when it came to her role; she emphasised quite how wonderful her new life was, too. 'Everyone here is really lovely and I enjoy being part of such a great soap,' she said. 'I'm also getting used to being recognised as well, it comes as part of the package, really. All the cast have a good time on the *EastEnders* set because we make each other laugh all the time.'

Her immediate success was noticed by the industry, too. In almost no time at all, she began to win awards, starting with Best Newcomer at the National British Soap Awards. There followed in quick succession more awards – *TV Quick* Awards for Best New Actress and the *Inside Soap* Award, also for best newcomer. 'I'm going to put it with my other two,' said an overwhelmed Jessie about the third of these. 'They've got pride of place in my living room.' It really was a phenomenal success in such a short time.

Despite the growing public recognition, and the acclaim from various awards panels, Jessie retained her down-to-earth qualities. She was modest about her contribution to the role of Kat, and gave much credit to the writers, directors and producers of *EastEnders*. 'She's such a strong character – and she's come in with such a bang,' she said. This was again a wise approach to take.

Time and again, soap opera stars have become enormously popular with the public, but then make the very great mistake of thinking that it is they, rather than their characters, who hold a place in the nation's heart. But, as so many have learnt to their cost, no one is bigger than the Square (or the Street). It is the wise actor or actress who understands that it is not just he or she who makes a role, but the innumerable others who work behind the scenes as well.

Jessie was showing every sign of understanding the reality of her new position, while talent played a large part, luck and the input of a great many other people had their place as well. But still she was wildly excited and thrilled by her new life – and who could blame her? To have drifted for years and then to wind up as a near-national treasure within a short time of embarking on a new career would be heady stuff for anyone. But when that career entails appearing on the nation's television screens several times a week, the excitement is greater still.

And this was just the beginning. Jessie was to discover that public interest in her merely seemed to grow as the years passed, and given that her personal life sometimes resembled a soap opera, too, that interest was not so unlikely. The British love people who are larger than life, and Jessie was to prove to be that off the set as well as on. She is one of those people who attracts drama and controversy and, given her outspokenness, continued to prompt plenty of both.

Her love life also became a national preoccupation. That was something Jessie certainly didn't expect; like most women, she'd had a number of boyfriends and, like most women, she was looking for Mr Right. The drama of her own personal human interest storyline seemed to match that of Kat's fictional life on screen, and there was little chance to escape public scrutiny. Indeed, many people could relate to what Jessie found herself going through, and just about everyone found it fascinating.

Perhaps that is the secret of being a real star – your private life is every bit as eventful as any a scriptwriter might have imagined and then placed on the screen. Jessie's was certainly to prove just as captivating.

4

Letting the Kat Out of the Bag

Private life aside, things were hotting up professionally, too, when Jessie was awarded one of the most explosive storylines in *EastEnders* to date. It caused an absolute sensation when it was aired – Kat was actually Zoë's mother, not her sister, and her uncle Harry, played by the late Michael Elphick, was the father. Kat had been just thirteen when she became pregnant and gave birth at fourteen, telling everyone the father was a boy from school.

'Those episodes were brilliantly written, and organisations like the NSPCC helped, so it was very well handled,' Jessie said. 'And Michael Elphick was such a lovely man and a great actor – I loved working with him. Of every single scene that I've done, my favourite one was when Kat confronted Harry.'

Even in this day and age, the storyline caused a

sensation. And it was difficult to play, as well. Just the right amount of emotion was needed, without sending the key scenes completely over the top. It would have been a challenge for an actress of long standing, but for one who had started as recently as Jessie, it could have been a major hurdle. In the event, she pulled it off to great acclaim, although she was well aware of what a challenge it would be.

'Really overwhelmed,' she said, when asked what her initial reaction would be. 'It went completely over my head. When it got closer to the scenes when we found out Kat was Zoë's mum, I was petrified that I wouldn't know how to do it. There were people out there it happened to – how was I going to make it look convincing?'

And Jessie was well aware of what a controversial twist this was to be. 'Kat adored her uncle Harry when she was younger,' she explained. 'She had a crush on him and used to follow him everywhere. When he started touching her, she knew deep down it wasn't right, but she didn't know how to react to it. She never told a soul that he's the father, except her mum. Her mum accused her of lying and so she didn't tell anyone else. It was very intense, but it's so brilliantly written that it was a joy to do. I love getting my scripts, because some of Kat's lines are so funny. She's strong, but she's also got a vulnerability to her.'

Indeed, telling everyone involved about the storyline also had to be handled with extreme care. Kat, Zoë and the Slaters might have been fictional characters, but they were tackling one of the last really big taboo subjects – the sexual abuse of children – and so it wouldn't have been natural if the actors had been completely untouched by the subject matter they were dealing with. Jessie, especially, had to take on board a difficult emotional role.

'The producer, John Yorke, called me into a meeting to tell me, but to be honest, I wasn't that surprised, because I already had an inkling it might have been something like that,' she said. 'For a girl to be pregnant at such a young age, and be so cagey about the whole thing… And then, when the character of Harry turned up, I had an inkling. Because every time he walked into a room Kat would literally flinch.'

This, incidentally, was not something written into the script; by this time, Jessie empathised with the character she played so well that she was able to improvise. 'It was just kind of "between the lines" and, to be honest, Kat's such a big part of my life and I know the character so well that you do start to… I just knew,' she said.

In fact, Jessie had been late to the relevant meeting, and learned after everyone else what path the storyline was to take. 'It wasn't until the first week of filming that we had this meeting,' she said. 'I was a bit late and everyone was sitting round this table. When I walked in it all went quiet. I sat down next to Elaine Lordan and she passed me this note which said, 'You're Zoë's mum'. I was like, "What?"'

There was then the challenge of not letting anyone know what was going to happen. That was made all the more difficult by the fact that some people came very close to guessing. 'I was getting letters from children saying, "You're Zoë's mum, aren't you?"' said Jessie. 'Children say a lot of things.'

The scenes took a fortnight to shoot and it was a wearing time for all. After it was over, Jessie flew to Majorca, but could not entirely forget the harrowing storyline. 'It wasn't until I had time to sit down and think that the strength of the storyline really hit me,' she said. 'I was trying to relax and it kept popping into my head. I had all these images of how and when it happened to Kat. I thought I'd be able to switch off from it, but I couldn't.

'I've already had letters from girls who have had teenage pregnancies, and I try to answer as many as I can. I just don't know what the media reaction will be when this goes out, or how viewers will react. But I think it's good that *EastEnders* is touching a powerful subject like this. Obviously, the circumstances are totally alien to me, but things like this really are happening. Hopefully, by exposing it, we can help the victims of such abuse in some kind of way.'

In fact, as Jessie later revealed, the nature of her fan mail changed quite a bit after that storyline. It was almost too much. After all, Jessie was an actress, not a psychologist, and the storyline had clearly awoken very sad memories in very many people. 'Up until then, I'd get a lot of letters from men about Kat's red boots – they've always been popular!' said Jessie. 'And children had always written lovely things to me. But after those episodes, I had loads of letters from kids who'd had similar experiences, confiding in me, and I didn't really know how to cope with that. Luckily, it was put in the hands of people who could deal with it. But the response changes depending on what's happening on screen – at the moment most of my mail is about Kat and Alfie Moon.'

Michelle Ryan, who played Zoë, was also well aware of what a contentious issue it would turn out to be, and what a toll it could take to play it. 'I knew a couple of months after joining the show that Zoë was going to turn out to be Kat's daughter, so I was always aware that it would be a big story, but I never knew quite what it would entail,' she said.

'When I was told Harry was going to be the father, I was incredibly shocked and thought, "No, they can't, they won't do that!" because you just don't want to think about something like this. I was worried about how the writers were going to do it because it's such a delicate and sensitive issue. It had to be handled with the utmost care and responsibility and not sensationalised at all.'

Indeed, Michelle was also taking on quite a burden with her own role. Still only seventeen, this was a very charged area in which to be working, and one that required the finest acting skills. She realised just how much depended on her being able to pull it off. 'It's a huge compliment to be given this responsibility, but I was very nervous and desperate to do the story justice,' she said. 'Hopefully, we will have, but it will be hard for some people to watch. I came out of the [preview] room crying. It's just such a sad story, a real emotional rollercoaster ride. It really does hit you.'

It helped that the two actresses got on extremely well together. 'I get on brilliantly with her... we work really well together, get a good buzz off each other and learn from each other,' said Michelle. 'I also watched films like *Boys Don't Cry* and *Girl, Interrupted* and you can draw a lot from similar cases to Zoë's that you read about and see in the media. Hopefully, she and Kat will be able to build something, but I don't think there's going to be a happy ending. To be honest, this is going to rip the Slater family apart.'

In the event, the scene was a resounding success. The morning after the relevant episode aired, Jessie was left in no doubt as to how her peers thought she'd done. 'I went into work the next day and there was bunches and bunches of flowers there for me,' she said. 'I got one off Pauline Quirke… a message off Sue Johnston. It was such a buzz!'

Jessie herself was aware that it was one of those moments in her career that she could be really proud of. 'My most favourite scene was when I confronted Uncle Harry, played by Michael Elphick, in the Square,' she said. 'I felt everything he'd done to Kat welling up inside me. I felt delirious, a year of pent-up emotion.' Even so, she had not lost the faculty for self-criticism. 'You always think you could have done a bit better,' she said, when asked how she felt after powerfully emotional scenes. 'It's quite a fast turnover at *EastEnders* so that's the way it works.'

It was quite an entrance to one of the most talked about and popular shows in the country. Kat had arrived with a bang and created more noise still, with the end result that the country was rooting both for her and the character she played. But did Jessie ever wonder what she was going to do next?

'Definitely,' said Jessie. 'When you film something as challenging as that in such an early stage of your *EastEnders* career, you do wonder where you go from there. You worry that you've peaked too soon. But I've had brilliant stuff since, like the miscarriage storyline.

It's great that my character's established now, but has stayed fresh. Kat's making different journeys all the time, so it's still exciting. And I love her working behind the bar in the Vic... being behind the bar is the best feeling in the world. I was looking at the picture of Angie Watts on the wall in there, and I thought, "I can't believe I'm standing where Anita Dobson used to stand." When I watched *EastEnders* as a kid, I never imagined in a million years that I'd be where she was one day.'

Storyline traumas apart, Jessie was also extremely good natured about her alter ego. While keen to maintain the differences between them, she was not averse to a bit of gentle self-mockery about the character that had made her name. 'Sometimes, I think I'm turning into Kat,' she said. 'The other day we were improvising and the director just said, "Say goodbye as if you're Kat." A year ago, I would have just said, "See ya," but I just came out with, "If you can't be good, be good at it." Afterwards I thought, "I'm turning into Kat."'

Jessie was now becoming really famous. Fortunately, however, she still had her three closest friends, who were able to keep her feet on the ground. One was Nicky Hood. 'We're so close we know everything about each other,' she said. 'We're like soul mates really.' The other two were Stuart and Keith, who had by now moved to Los Angeles. 'I really miss them,' said Jessie in 2001. 'I shot out there for a week recently to see them and it was great, because I've always wanted to go there. They live by the Santa Monica pier and they took me to the Hollywood Hills and I saw all the things I've only seen on TV.'

It was a much needed way of staying close to reality. The sensational storyline, involving Kat and Zoë, had made Jessie more famous still. Appearing on *EastEnders* would have guaranteed press exposure whatever the character anyone played, but to be central to one of the most high-profile twists in the programme's history made those at the centre of it all the more fascinating to public and press alike.

Interest in Jessie continued to grow and, along with it, increasing numbers of interviews and articles about her. Much of this was completely harmless. Asked if she believed in the afterlife, she replied, 'I do, yeah. Do you ever get the feeling when you're walking down a street and you just know that you've been there before? Every day, since you ask. Usually when I pass my own house... If I had to come back to life as an insect, I'd come back as a butterfly. If it was a bird, I'd like to come back as a raven. I do like ravens. It's the way they walk around, like they've got an attitude.'

There was a good deal more where this came from. How would she describe herself in a lonely hearts ad?

'"Raven-like ice maiden with nutty sense of humour seeks gent." I do have quite a nutty sense of humour. People falling over — that always makes me laugh. Though I wouldn't laugh if I saw someone fall off a building. It's more the slapstick thing.'

Her sexual fantasy? 'I'd love to have sex in the thunder in a field thick with mud. With a man in a top hat.' And what was her favourite food? 'I love meat. Except for lamb, 'cos it smells too much like an animal. I don't like to be reminded that I'm eating an animal. Which is why I like my steaks well done. I'm more of a meat person than a biscuit person, though I'd never go in for cannibalism. I'd sooner gnaw my own leg than someone else's.'

More searching questions — her feelings about cheese? 'I like cheese, especially Stilton, though I wouldn't want to drive a car made out of Stilton. But cheese is great. If I buy a massive lump of cheese, I have to finish it there and then. So I only buy it in small amounts. Otherwise I'd be as big as a house. A house made of cheese. That's a nice image to finish on, don't you think?'

But, as Jessie very soon found out, there is a downside to fame as well, and if you have been catapulted into it as quickly as she had, that downside can be even more shocking. Bosses at the BBC had warned her about it and encouraged her to own up to any problems in the past but Jessie, like so many others before her, had not fully realised what this would mean in practice. It was not long before the papers found out about the conviction relating to drink-driving.

Jessie was open about the good appearing alongside the bad. Asked if there were downsides to fame at all, she replied, 'Not being able to go out in my nightdress. I can't pop to the shop with no make-up on any more. The only annoying thing really is when everyone kept saying I had a big bum – one paper said I had to prise myself out of a car. Another said I should cut back on the PVC because I'm beginning to look like a walking sofa. I laughed at first, but I got a bit upset. They can be very personal. And there was a picture of me picking up dog poo – that wasn't very flattering!'

But the upside of her new life more than made up for any aggro she might have had. Jessie was still behaving much like a child in a sweet shop, utterly delighted and yet bemused by the good fortune that had come her way. She was, on the whole, thoroughly enjoying her fame and, now that she was getting used to being recognised, she was beginning to enjoy that, too. 'In Tesco earlier today, these kids followed me down every aisle,' she related in one interview. 'Every time I glanced back at them, they all looked at their shoes. They were so sweet. And the other day, these two boys were fidgeting on the street. I walked past and they stopped and shouted, "Kat!" It's nice to know they like her so much.'

Then there was the feeling in some quarters that she was taking to her new role in life with a little more gusto than she should. Jessie had gone almost overnight from being a complete unknown to being extremely famous, and had had little time to learn how to deal with the constant interest that was shown in her by the press. She also, for the first time in her life, had some money. She joined *EastEnders* on a salary thought to be about £80,000 a year, which was vastly more than she had been used to. Her salary also began to rise as she grew increasingly successful, and is now thought to be about £250,000 a year.

All of this meant she was free to indulge herself, and she did. Jessie had always liked a drink and, still not entirely aware of where these high jinks could lead her, was photographed looking rather the worse for wear, dancing around in the streets. The pictures duly made it into the papers, leading to a furore, with the powers that be on *EastEnders* said to be distinctly unamused. 'That picture's haunting me!' she said, shortly after it was taken, by which time she had fully taken on board all the problems it could cause.

'I'd just been to an *EastEnders* party and I was a bit merry when I came out, so I started doing the can-can and mucking around. I think I did the one finger salute, too! It upset me a bit when I saw the picture – but it could have been worse. It taught me a lesson, though. I haven't been out since! I got a few nasty letters from people afterwards. One person sent a copy of the picture with a letter telling me I was a disgrace. I don't know what to say to that – I was dancing and enjoying myself!' But she had been affected by the fuss that was caused. 'Well, I can't have a good drink like I used to, because I don't know who's watching,' she confessed. 'All it takes is for me to trip over and fall flat on my face and it'll be all over the papers.'

Jessie was also beginning to realise that her new life was having an effect on her family. She did a picture shoot for the magazine *Loaded*, in which she lived up to the sex siren image by posing provocatively in a state of semi-undress. This did not go down well with her parents. 'My mum told me off a few months ago when I did the *Loaded* shoot and was on the cover of the magazine with my bra strap hanging down,' she confessed, sounding for all the world like a defensive teenager. 'She wasn't too happy!' It was not, however, a serious complaint.

But Jessie really was beginning to discover that fame came at a price, and that private matters, such as her personal life, were soon going to be the matter for national debate. Her boyfriends have made headlines pretty much from the time that Jessie herself has been doing so, and none more so than the man she had been dating when she first started in *EastEnders*. His name? Paul Whitworth.

She had been denying it for months, but at last the truth was out. Jessie Wallace had a boyfriend: Paul Whitworth, a businessman living in Majorca, who was not only much older than her – by seventeen years – but who had a decidedly chequered past. In 1971, he had served eighteen months in prison for cheque fraud and, worse still, seven years later he was subject to ten charges of armed robbery. In the event, by the time the trial began at the Old Bailey in 1980, there was only one charge to answer, and the jury failed to reach a verdict. Paul was found not guilty by direction of the judge. But, still, this was a bit of a shock, given that Jessie was fast becoming the nation's favourite soap actress.

The two, it emerged, had been together for two years, since well before Jessie had started to appear in *EastEnders*. And now the secret was out, there was nothing to do except be completely up-front about it. Jessie explained that they first met when she worked in a pub. 'When I used to work in The Oak, he used to come in and, mmmm, it was love at first sight,' she said. 'He is very gorgeous. I really was hooked straight away and I've never had that.'

It was not, however, as Jessie was keen to emphasise,

an overly serious relationship. After all, he lived in another country, for a start. 'He does live in Spain,' said Jessie. 'He's got his life over there and I've got mine, but we're very close. It's never been really serious. We don't live in each other's pockets, we've both got our own lives. That's why we get on so well.'

But what, Jessie was tentatively asked, about his criminal past? Some papers had been saying that she was being sucked into a life of crime and horror; what was the real truth? Jessie laughed it off. 'Really? Sucked into a life of crime and horror? There's no crime and no horror. They must be thinking of Albert Square. My friends were very amused by the stories in the papers and so was I.'

The two were, however, definitely an ongoing couple. Jessie revealed that Paul had been over for the National Television Awards, although, 'He watched it in my front room because I'd promised to take my little sister. He's very private and we didn't want to be out there for all the photographers.'

Indeed, by this time, Jessie was definitely getting tired of at least some of the attention. When it first began she was thrilled – as most people would be – but, by now, she was beginning to wish for some privacy at least. 'I obviously understand that it's part and parcel of what I do, but nevertheless it's hard to get used to because I'm quite a private person,' she said of the constant attention she now got from the press. 'It's strange that they're printing parts of your life that you wouldn't even think people would be interested in. All I want to do is do my job and go home. I knew it would be a bit like this, but I didn't expect people to be camping outside my house.'

As if all that were not enough, reports then surfaced that the bailiffs had been knocking at Jessie's door. It was beginning to seem as if her life was every bit as eventful as her fictional alter ego, and she was plainly getting a little fed up. 'I wasn't aware of them coming round at all,' she protested. 'I wasn't in. When I was in drama school, I got into a bit of debt, but as far as I'm aware I've paid it off, so I don't know what all that's about.'

Her new life did, however, have its compensations. She was mixing with the stars, appearing on the likes of Graham Norton's chat show – alongside Cher – and gaining admiration from her peers. 'Pauline Quirk sent me a big bunch of flowers after the big two-hander and Sue Johnston sent me a letter,' she said. 'She's lovely. Paul O'Grady, I bumped into him a while ago. It's funny when people you've loved on TV for years come up to you and say they think you're good. Graham Norton watches. Cher watched it as well. When she told me, I just went, "Great," and thought, "I don't believe you." She's really funny, though.'

And, all the trauma aside, the BBC was determined to

hang on to its new star. Jessie signed a new contract with them for an unspecified amount, and was able to indulge herself in more clothes. Asked if she was a label snob, she replied, 'No, I've got a few bits, but I love vintage clothes. I love Gucci and Prada and Yves St Laurent. That suit I wore for the TV awards, Paul bought me, and that's the most expensive item of clothing I've got.'

Indeed, Jessie was becoming such a style icon that she was regularly asked about her beauty regime, questions that she was prepared to answer with enthusiasm. 'Estée Lauder Nutri Resilience is my favourite,' she said. 'My skin has been so much better since I've been using it. It's very rich and there's an eye cream to go with it.'

Unsurprisingly, another favourite was a tanning product. 'I'm a fan of St Tropez fake tan, too,' said Jessie. 'I apply it myself and I prefer the mud, not the instant mousse. I've been using it for a while now. I love being tanned, personally, but I go that little bit extra brown for Kat. I used to be a sun worshipper, but I'm not any more. I can't lay out in the sun these days, because I get bad pigmentation on my face. I've been getting them for the past couple of years.'

Jessie was also asked if she'd consider plastic surgery. 'Definitely!' she said. 'I would have my nose straightened, because it took a bit of a knock when I was younger, which caused a bit of a bump. It used to be really straight. It's bent now and I really notice it. If it didn't cause two black eyes, I'd have the op tomorrow. Apparently, the girl who won a Kat Slater lookalike competition said something like, "I look exactly like Kat, even down to the bump on her nose." I'm already obsessed with it, so that just made it worse! I'd do something about my lip, as well, because it goes up on one side where I've chewed half of it away. I don't like my feet, either. I hate my own feet and everyone else's, too.'

As for clothes, Jessie was in her element. Always a stylish woman, she now had the wherewithal to build up her wardrobe, and was relishing every minute of it. 'I shop in all different kinds of clothes shops and I do like some designer clothes, but I don't wear my labels on the outside,' she said. 'I've got a shoe and handbag fetish, though – I think I've got about seventy of each!'

The fuss eventually died down but, if truth be told, there were still worries in the background. The BBC had seen enough soap stars come unstuck before now to be aware of the dangers that could befall them, on top of which was a growing feeling that they didn't want to lose Jessie. She was showing herself to be a superb actress, handling very difficult story lines with aplomb – and this after she had only just started acting – and there was a growing feeling that Jessie might be able to do more for the BBC than simply appear as Kat. There was an increasing amount riding on her and no one around her wanted her to trip up.

And it must be said, her feet still seemed firmly on the ground. Having been in the show for just one year and already being rewarded with a clutch of awards, Jessie still seemed quite overawed by it all. 'I still can't believe what's happened in the last year,' she said. 'I get up and walk into the kitchen every morning and I've got the awards on my windowsill. I just sort of stop and look at them!'

She was delightfully open about many aspects of her life, too, which continued to win her increasing numbers of fans. Girls, in particular, could empathise with her continuing absorption in clothes and make-up. Asked if she wore make-up every day, she replied, 'Yes. I don't wear as much as Kat, but I do like a bit of foundation, mascara and lipstick. I always wear that much, even on days when I'm not doing much.' And perfume? 'Must by Cartier is my favourite for the day,' said Jessie. 'I've been wearing it for fifteen years. I like Bulgari for the evening.'

Of course, it helped that she had been a make-up artist. Jessie knew how to transform not only other people's appearances, but her own, a talent she used to great effect. 'The best thing was shading and highlighting, which enables you to do things like make big noses look smaller or chubby noses look slimmer,' she confided.

Her female fans loved it. Any fellow woman who was very aware of imperfections in her appearance and completely able to talk about them without seeming neurotic appeals enormously to girls (and women) and she was deeply self-deprecating about it, too. Asked if she exercised, she replied, 'Only by walking my shih-tzu, Bailey. I normally walk him twice a day. He's very energetic – especially when he's had a haircut – he springs about everywhere.

'I want to join a gym, but I've never been to one before. I bought all the Reebok gear in preparation, but it's all still lying in my bedroom in the packets. I bought a sit-up machine the other day, but it took me so long to put it together, I was exhausted by the time I finished! I think I probably need a personal trainer, but I'm too lazy to get one.' As ever, she was speaking the language her many fans could understand.

5

Man Hunt

Jessie was now beginning to think about other aspects of her life, too. She was now in her early thirties and, having finally found a career path she really wanted, she was beginning to think about what else was important in her life. Her sister Joanne had five children by now and Jessie was getting very accustomed to the joys of being an aunt, but did she want more than that?

The answer was yes. She was now at a stage when many women decide that it might be the ideal time to start a family. And it was quite feasible; soap operas are often written around the real-life dramas of those who star in them, and so her job would not necessarily be jeopardised. Indeed, in an interview, Jessie was asked whether she ever felt broody. 'Yes, I'd really love to have children,' she said firmly. 'That feeling has just come out of nowhere – I've found myself just drooling over kids.'

She was to get her wish, but not just yet, for the problem was that she still had not found the right father for her child. Her relationship with Paul was faltering, and so this was not the ideal time to start thinking about having a baby. And she still had a few controversies to overcome before she finally did get round to giving birth.

If truth be told, Jessie was entering a period in which she didn't look much as if she wanted to be settling down. She was still not entirely used to the idea that public interest in her was such that everything she did and said would be monitored from now on. She was to suffer, somewhat, from this interest as well, for while her actions might have mirrored those of many a high-spirited young woman, the majority of those women don't actually end up in the papers. And so began the first in a series of problems and allegations that were, ultimately, to lead her BBC bosses to take a very serious course of action with their latest star name.

There were several factors at play here which contributed to the problem. First there was the issue of overnight success, never easy for anyone to handle. Jessie simply wasn't used to all the attention. Then there was her own temperament – volatile, fiery and slightly prone to putting her foot in it. And then there were her fellow cast members or, to be more accurate, the fellow new cast members.

All wildly excited by their success, their growing profile and the fact that they had risen from obscurity to become household names practically overnight, they perhaps egged one another on a little more than was healthy or desirable. Whatever the reason, little hiccups turned into bigger ones. Life was imitating the soap opera's art and it could have had major repercussions for Jessie, had she not, at the very last moment, edged back from the brink.

The first really serious escapade came about at the end of 2001, when Jessie was said to have hit a cab driver, after he drove her and her friends home after a night out at the pub. The Muslim cab driver alleged that she had been calling him 'Osama bin Laden' the whole way home but, once there, matters got completely out of hand and an extended row ensued which, of course, got into the press. She had hailed Joynal Abddin's cab outside the Royal Oak in Loughton, Essex, her old stamping ground, but was said to have reacted with astonishment when she was told what she would have to pay.

Mr Abddin was reported to have said, 'She'd obviously had a good night out and was quite merry. Throughout the journey she kept calling me "bin

Laden". I found it offensive, but you get used to it when people have had a few drinks, so I said nothing. But when I told her how much she had to pay, she went utterly ballistic and slapped me across the face. I was shocked.

'I couldn't believe what she'd done. She stormed out of my car and refused to pay. I said I didn't make the rules and wanted my money. Eventually, one of her friends handed over the cash. If you think that Kat Slater is a bit of a scrapper, you should see Jessie Wallace in full flight.'

Jessie utterly denied all of these allegations.

It was all very unfortunate, and that was not the end of it. Joynal made a complaint to the police, his cab company banned Jessie from using the firm and Jessie threatened to sue over the bill. She also denied hitting anyone. Joynal stood his ground. 'I knew who she was straight away,' he said. 'She was dressed all in black in a revealing top and baggy trousers and was wearing lots of make-up.'

The problem, it appeared, was two-fold; all the taxi firms in the area were charging double for the period over Christmas and the New Year, on top of which, according to Joynal, five friends were with her and each had to be dropped off home.

'If I'd driven her from the pub to her flat, the fare wouldn't have been so expensive,' said Joynal. 'But I had to make several detours to take her friends home. I know £50 sounds a lot, but I don't make the rules. If you don't want to pay for a cab, don't hire it. I can handle being called a few names. However, I refuse to be hit. Just because she's famous, she thinks she can get away with this kind of behaviour. Well... she can't.'

Whatever the truth of the incident, it was not a happy episode and was the first sign that real ructions could occur in Jessie's career. She needed to learn that her private life was now of great interest to the public and that there were going to be repercussions because she was no longer just an anonymous face in the street. And not only was she famous, but children saw her as their idol and role model as well.

Shortly after this incident, there was more turmoil in her life when her relationship with Paul Whitworth became increasingly rocky. It was a shame; whatever he might have done in the past, the two were clearly very attached to one another and he appears to have been her most successful relationship to date. But, alas, it was not going well. 'I saw them together in January,' said one observer, a couple of months on. 'They were out shopping for jeans and seemed huffy with each other. There was no body contact at all and she was off talking on her mobile all the time. I believe they had quite an intense relationship.'

It must be said that was not untypical of the way they

behaved towards each other. The two had never been all over each other in public; they conducted their relationship very much away from the public gaze. 'We used to see Jessie and Paul on the terrace of a bar called Wellies a lot,' said Humphrey Carter of the *Majorcan Daily Bulletin* in April 2002. 'Last summer, she practically lived over here with him. Although, if you didn't know them, you would never have thought they were a couple. They were very private and never wanted to have their picture taken together.'

Perhaps inevitably, it soon emerged that Jessie had indeed split up with Paul. There was a lot of speculation as to what had prompted this. Whatever the real reason, the romance was at an end. More likely was the fact that Paul simply didn't like the publicity that surrounded a relationship with a television personality. After all, when he'd first met Jessie, she had been a complete unknown. He did not relish the spotlight in this particular case and that cannot have been good for the health of the relationship.

Neither, of course, did the distance between them help. Paul lived in Majorca, Jessie lived in London and, no matter how often they flew across to be with one another, they really were leading two separate lives. Jessie was also so much busier than she had been previously. Apart from a hectic filming schedule, she was becoming increasingly sought after for photo shoots and showbusiness parties and awards ceremonies. Her life was accelerating, which made the relationship more difficult to keep up with than ever before.

Neither was it obvious that their future lay in the same direction. Now that she had tasted success, Jessie wished to have more of it; she did not want to leave the stage now that it was finally her turn to act. That also, clearly, ruled out any permanent move to Majorca. Nonetheless, the break-up of the relationship clearly left her a little emotionally raw, however.

Jessie took it philosophically. 'We split up because it just wasn't working out,' she said. 'I always seem to go for the wrong kind of blokes. I do want to find someone who is sweet, considerate and makes me laugh – that would be my perfect man. But I don't tend to meet them because people have the wrong impression of me – they think I'm exactly like Kat. I think I have a type, and that's the problem. I go for tall, dark men and the cheeky types.'

For once, Jessie appeared to be a little less than her usual bubbly, positive self. A fighter at the best of times, it is extremely rare to have seen her sounding wistful, but that was the way she was acting after the split from Paul, even if she did struggle to put a brave face on it all. 'I'm happy to be single now… I can eye up the men when I'm out,' said Jessie. 'I should look at dating the nice, quiet ones, but they usually turn out to be the worst sort in the long run, anyway.' It certainly sounded as if she was feeling a bit low.

That was not the only comment she made on the subject. The famous, like the rest of us, can have problems in their love lives, and Jessie was feeling a bit bruised. On another occasion she remarked, 'I'm sick of men. The last thing I want now is another relationship. People warned me about his [Paul's] colourful past and told me to stay away, but I didn't take any notice. Men I meet all think I am just like Kat Slater. I love Kat to bits, but I am not like that in real life. A lot of men think I am this slapper who doesn't want a real relationship.'

The blurring between fact and fiction was clearly getting to be a bit much. And although she might not have felt like getting together with a new boyfriend at that exact moment, there was the issue of broodiness. Jessie's maternal instincts were beginning to make themselves felt, and so, subconsciously or otherwise, she was not just in the running for a new boyfriend if she started dating anyone else, but a potential father for her future children, too.

Matters weren't helped by a change of personnel in Albert Square. Jessie had become very used to what was becoming her second home and so, when there were upheavals professionally, it upset her personally, too. A number of important figures were leaving, including

Martin Kemp and Tamzin Outhwaite, which created a slightly uneasy atmosphere for the rest of the cast, simply because the dynamics of their workplace had changed and people they had grown close to weren't going to be there any longer. Jessie, however, was adamant that she wasn't going to join the exodus. 'I'm staying put for now,' she said. 'I have no plans to leave.'

It would have been surprising if she'd said anything different. It sounds contradictory to say that Jessie was both very famous and still establishing herself, but that was indeed the case. Because her career had taken off so quickly, she didn't have a big body of acting work to fall back on, and was still in some ways learning her new trade and showing the rest of the showbusiness world just what she was capable of. The last thing she wanted to do just as her career was becoming stratospheric was to leave the show that put her there in the first place. And the BBC didn't want her to go, either. It knew it had a major star on its hands.

A brief fling followed, which might have helped to cheer her up. Jessie was seen out dating club boss Ben Heath after meeting him at his club, Catch 22. Normally a straight club, it was hosting a gay evening and fellow clubbers were slightly astonished when Jessie stood up and yelled, 'Is there anyone here who isn't fucking gay?' Ben politely introduced himself, invited her for a private drink and, very briefly, the two became an item. At least it helped take her mind off other things.

But this one certainly wasn't to last. 'Jessie is really fond of Ben and had lots of fun with him, but it was starting to show signs of getting serious and she didn't really feel up to it,' said a friend. 'Ben really liked her and they had a real laugh together but Jessie doesn't want to be tied down so soon. She hadn't been single for long after breaking up with Paul and she feels awful about the situation. It's a shame because she really likes Ben, but it was simply a case of bad timing.'

And so it was back to being single again. Jessie said she didn't mind. 'I like to have my bed to myself,' she said. 'Because I don't get out much, I don't really meet blokes. And I don't get loads of blokes chatting me up anyway, it's always idiots who say, "Oh look, it's Kat, she's up for a good time." At the moment, I'm happily single. I was in a relationship for three years but I'm not looking for anyone now. I'd love to be a mum one day, not yet, though. Hopefully, I'll meet the right person and settle down, but at the moment I'm keeping my head down.'

In truth, Jessie had been trying to forget Paul in that tried and tested fashion – by finding a new man. The split was actually affecting her more than she initially let on, with increasing reports of drinking sessions and raucous behaviour, in what was quite clearly a bid to block out what was upsetting her. It was hardly surprising that she was feeling a little blue. She and Paul had been an item for some years, and it had clearly been a serious relationship. And so, in another time-honoured way, she would have a few drinks too many to blot out the hurt.

This, again, raised eyebrows at the BBC, but as long as nothing too serious occurred, Jessie could just about get away with it. It also helped when she won the *Maxim* Woman of the Year Award, leading to more publicity, this time all of it favourable. It also provided concrete proof of the affection she was held in by the public. Then, however, reports of another row emerged, this one with far more serious consequences.

The scene was early 2002 and the setting was BBC1's 2001 TV Moments party. As usual, everyone had been drinking too much and Jessie became embroiled in a furious row with a fellow guest. Hannah Waterman, daughter of Dennis Waterman and one of Jessie's co-stars on *EastEnders*, saw what was happening, and tried to break up the fight.

It was not a good move. Jessie – allegedly – turned around and slapped her in the face. It was then said that Hannah's boyfriend Ricky Groves, who plays Garry Hobbs in *EastEnders*, had to step in to stop it from escalating into something uglier still, helped by various shocked onlookers. According to witnesses, Jessie then fled to the loos in tears, with Laila Morse, who plays her grandmother, Mo. Laila looked after her until order was restored.

In public relations terms, this did not go down well. The scene, unsurprisingly, made yet more headlines. One newspaper reported, 'It was amazing. Hannah was furious and wanted to have a go back, while Laila was just like her character, Big Mo, protecting the tearful Slater girls. It was like watching a scene from *EastEnders*.' It was much worse than that, actually – for this was real life.

The BBC was not amused. A spokesman stiffly confirmed that there had been words between the two women at the party, but that was all. 'It was a private conversation,' she said. 'Jessie absolutely didn't hit Hannah and Hannah confirmed that also.' Various accusations and counter accusations were bandied about; what no one denied was that an altercation had taken place, and a very fierce one at that. And while tensions between stars on the same show are not unknown, this one had erupted so publicly that there was little anyone could do to calm down the fuss.

Hannah, unsurprisingly, was livid. Relations reached glacial proportions between the two actresses and Jessie's reputation took a further knock. Hannah did not immediately comment on what had happened, but she didn't need to, given what a fuss everyone else was making of it. It would, in fact, be several months before she finally discussed publicly the row that had taken place.

Jessie herself was clearly very upset by the furore. 'We had a disagreement,' she said. 'But that's as far as it went. Unfortunately, there were journalists at the party, and they blew it out of all proportion. There were no fists or slapping. We're friends, but we had a disagreement.' But it was too late – the story had already run out of control.

A propensity for getting into trouble aside, Jessie's new life was throwing up other issues as well, not all of them bad. Some, in fact, were positively pleasurable. Whatever her other problems, she was now undeniably a sex symbol. Websites devoted to her were beginning to appear, and she appeared on the cover of magazines more regularly than ever.

Men who met her, famous or otherwise, were only too keen to extol her charms, while more women than ever aspired to look like her. There may be many downsides to being in showbusiness, but there are upsides, too, and this was one of them. And the press were certainly complimentary about this facet of her life, regularly commending her on her appearance, calling her stunning. Admittedly, they were also prone to teasing her for wearing too much fake tan! It was a new image that was growing and got bigger still when she was named sexiest female at an awards ceremony.

The lady herself was bemused by it all. 'I think…
urrrggghh… what's happened?' she said, when asked
for her thoughts on looking in the mirror every
morning. 'That's why it was such a shock to be voted
sexiest female at the British Soap Awards. A real shock,
but it's so flattering. I don't know whether it's Kat or
me, but either way it's great! It's funny, though, because
I've always been a bit of a tomboy.'

She might have been bemused, but no one else was.
The secret of her popularity was extremely easy to work
out; women empathised with her (or Kat) and men
fancied her. Jessie had never been short of male
attention, but now she was getting it on a national scale,
all of which, of course, was very good news for the soap
opera that she worked on. Not all publicity was good
publicity, but this aspect, at least, was going her way.

And in many ways, this was groundbreaking, because
Jessie was pretty much the first home-grown sex
symbol *EastEnders* had ever produced. There had been
plenty of major female characters, starting with Angie
Watts, but she was much more a strong character
actress than anything else. And, indeed, there were
people who had been sex symbols also in the show,
most notably Barbara Windsor. Actually, in many ways,
Barbara Windsor still is a sex symbol, but that does
rather pre-date the show.

But Jessie was the first actress ever to capture the

nation in quite that way, who had made her name by starring in the show. Not that she didn't have competition – the rest of the Slater sisters were also going down very well with the viewing population, especially the male half. She still, however, clearly had the edge.

The great irony, though, is that the better you look on television, the greater the pressure to maintain that image. And Jessie was beginning to feel the strain of maintaining her appearance. Some unkind observers had pointed out that she had gained a bit of weight. Others pointed out that her fake tan was turning a touch orange. Jessie laughed it off. 'People have to take me as they find me,' she said. 'I certainly don't feel like any kind of sex symbol.'

But she was working to look the part, and she was very conscious of her figure. 'I've put on a stone-and-a-half since I joined *EastEnders*,' she said. 'When I first started, I was tiny. I was size eight – I'm only five-foot one. I used to wear these jeans that sat on my hips and now I can't get my legs in them! You're sitting round all day sometimes and I just start snacking.' That, of course, is an element to film and television that can be lost to a wider audience. It can be a little tedious sitting around all day in between takes, and the temptation was to indulge in habits that were bad for you. With Jessie, it was nibbling too much.

She acknowledged it, too. '[I eat] savoury things… I haven't got a sweet tooth,' she said. 'I've been on a diet for the last few days. I make my own soup and eat steamed chicken and vegetables. I've got this exercise DVD. I bought it, watched it once and put in back in the box. I need to take my two dogs [by this time, Bailey had a friend] for long walks.'

Indeed, although she had always talked frankly about how much she hated the gym, she knew that she now had to keep in shape. Jessie became increasingly conscious about what and how much she was eating, and attempted to do some exercise as painlessly as possible. It is well known quite how much pressure is put on actresses to keep themselves slim and Jessie was feeling it, too. It was something else that was new to her – having to watch her weight – and she didn't always enjoy it. But it was all part of the price that had to be paid for television success.

On the man front, there was still little movement. Her name had been linked, usually falsely, to all manner of possible suitors, including Paul Trueman, Gary Beadle, Alistair McGowan and the DJ Brandon Block. Sometimes it was a bit wearisome. 'I don't want to have a relationship,' said Jessie, although it didn't seem to be entirely clear whether she was talking about herself or her on-screen alter ego.

'I want a trophy cabinet, thank you. I don't really

thrive on relationships. Kat lives for flings. And I'd like many more in the near future. I hope I have another fling with someone. Definitely. I don't think I am getting enough men. I mean, she is getting enough men. It's about time Kat ran a bit riot.' Kat, as it happens, didn't need much encouragement; she continued to cause quite as much havoc on screen as Jessie did off screen. The fictional Kat and Jessie, who played her, were, in truth, quite a strong-willed pair.

And, in the background, stresses and strains and the problems of fame aside, Jessie's career was gaining yet further momentum. She had been given some very difficult plotlines on *EastEnders*, and had managed to convince with no problem at all. Her range was proving to be extensive; she could do comedy (not that there was much of that in Kat's life) and drama, and make every scene she appeared in believable. And this was important, not just for her work in *EastEnders*, but for her future, too.

The powers that be at the BBC were not watching Jessie merely to see how well she acted in Albert Square, or whether she misbehaved in her personal life. They were also watching to judge her longer-term potential, and they liked what they saw. Soap operas can sometimes be a breeding ground for great talent – just look at Sarah Lancashire, who first made her name playing the dippy barmaid Raquel in *Coronation Street* –

and, increasingly, the Beeb was becoming convinced that, in Jessie, it had a real talent on its hands. Not that it was saying so publicly. Jessie was still very much the eager young soap star, prone to unfortunate decision-making at times, and had to be handled with care.

It was to be a while before the relationship between Jessie and the BBC settled down, because she still managed to cause havoc everywhere she went. Looking back, it actually taught her a valuable lesson, even if it didn't appear to her like that at the time. The bigger the star, the more controversy they can get away with causing – but no one, no matter how big a name, can step over a certain invisible line. And that is a lesson the wise star learns quickly, as Jessie, ultimately, was going to do.

That era was still ahead and, indeed, although she's avoided the kind of headlines in recent years that appeared with such regularity back then, she is still very much a character who provokes headlines. Fittingly, she really is larger than life; every relationship caused fresh dramas, and everywhere she goes, to this day, she continues to make news. That is clearly not her fault; the press and the public love it when they meet a true original and, in Jessie, they had certainly found that.

But still, she couldn't cross that invisible line. Jessie had to learn to calm herself, to remember that she was constantly in the public eye, to present an image that was lively, certainly, but one that never went too far.

And if there was the odd slip? Jessie is Jessie. Part of her phenomenal popularity rests upon the fact that she's human, like the rest of us, and not always totally in control of her life. She has ups and down like anyone and the public love her all the more for it. And besides – no one can be absolutely perfect all the time.

6

Life Through a Lens

The constant attention was now really beginning to take its toll – Jessie wouldn't have been human if it hadn't done so. She had achieved the breakthrough that so many actors and actresses dream of, but it did come at a price. The old Jessie, one who could mess around with her mates, had been replaced by a new Jessie, who was increasingly cautious about how she came across in public. And, sometimes, she missed her old, anonymous life. 'They give you a talk before you start on *EastEnders* about what to expect, but no one can prepare you for that,' she said. 'You wouldn't believe it if they told you, anyway. You've got to learn it for yourself. You get the odd lager lout that shouts something crude, but they're not talking to me, they're talking to Kat. I used to feel paranoid. Now I'd worry if I didn't get noticed! It's flattering. It's lovely when people say you were really good in that scene or you made me cry. I think, wow, that's a really big compliment.'

And, of course, the British have a funny take on celebrity. All sorts of attitudes emerge – envy, the wish to take someone down a peg or two, a misguided sense of actually knowing the person involved, respect, fascination – anything other than indifference. For a breed of people too cool to be impressed by anything, the British are remarkably apt to become tongue tied or, far worse, abusive when someone famous appears on the scene. And what is rarely discussed is how difficult it can be to be on the receiving end of all this. People who are famous are, after all, still people, and it is no easier for the Jessie Wallaces of this world to live under the very conflicting demands we make on our celebrities than it is for anyone else.

Jessie was beginning to appreciate this. She might have wanted to be famous, but only when she became so did she begin to understand the pressures involved. But then, of course, there was the huge upside, as well. She was beginning to live in a style she could only have dreamed of formerly; she now had a nice place to live in, a nice car and a lovely wardrobe. Being famous had its bonuses.

She did, however, laugh at suggestions that her life was glamorous. 'I was shopping in the supermarket the other day and this girl came up to me and said, "What are you doing in here?" I said, "Shopping... I have got legs."' It was a good illustration of the ambiguous attitude of the British towards the famous; Jessie would have been accused of pretension if she hadn't done her own shopping, and yet was regarded as somehow slumming it when she did. It is a very hard mix to get right.

As for luxuries, Jessie was adamant that she was not getting swept away by her new-found status. 'Posh food at the supermarket!' she said, when asked what her indulgences were. 'I buy designer clothes occasionally, but I still "um" and "ah" before forking out.' That, too, was a sensible attitude; she was making a determined effort both to stay normal and to portray herself as normal. It would have been a big mistake to start adopting airs and graces and Jessie was determined not to fall into that trap.

But her personal life was still going through difficulties. Jessie was pictured with Paul months after they had split up. They looked a lot more than just friends; they were caught in a passionate embrace, although, ultimately, they did not re-establish their relationship. 'She never got over Paul,' said a friend. 'Jessie always said he was the one man who made her feel truly happy. They met up in Majorca earlier this month when she was filming *EastEnders*. She was on the phone non-stop to Paul, begging him to come over. One reason they split up was that his mug would keep appearing in the papers. He'd prefer to stay out of the limelight.'

Jessie herself was quite upfront about how she felt. 'I still love him, despite the split,' she said. 'We talk on the phone a lot, but we've got different lives now. I'm not thinking about anyone else at the moment. I'm still getting over Paul. It's hard to trust people now and, when the time comes for me to start dating people again, I won't be going out with anyone unless they're in the same business as me.

'I meet people who have the wrong impression of me because they think I'm exactly like Kat.' Sometimes, fame can be difficult to deal with. Jessie Wallace had certainly learned the truth of that.

It was becoming increasingly clear to Jessie that fame threw up another problem that she previously hadn't anticipated. On the one hand, some men made the mistake of thinking that Jessie really was Kat, and so Jessie herself was not always quite sure as to which woman they were really pursuing. The public rarely think about this, or how difficult life can sometimes become for the celebrity. Is a potential suitor interested in them for the person they are in real life, or are they responding to the fictional image presented on screen? Then there was the issue common to all celebrities – did her admirers really like her for who she was, or did they glory in her reflected fame?

'I get a lot of very rude comments from men in the street, but I find that quite funny now,' said Jessie. 'They think I'll be just like Kat, but when I actually chat to them they realise I'm not, and they're sometimes disappointed by that. And I'm a bit disappointed that they're disappointed!'

It is sometimes hard to take celebrity complaints about their 'difficult' lifestyle very seriously, but it is absolutely true that many have to cope with pressures the vast majority of people simply don't have to bear. It is often difficult to judge another person's motives when establishing a relationship; how much more challenging must it be when fame enters the equation as well?

'Yeah, it definitely changes things,' Jessie said of her new-found fame. 'You're never sure if blokes only want to be with you because of the job you do, so you do put this barrier up. But, at the moment, I'm happy on my own.'

Indeed, that speculation about Jessie's love life was continuing to excite many. Jessie decided it was time to set the record straight. She had been linked with the DJ Brandon Block – was that true? 'No!' said Jessie. 'We met through Charlie Brookes [who plays Janine Butcher], and we went out for a meal with her and her boyfriend Tony. So because we looked like we were on a double date, it got blown out of proportion.

'Brandon's just a good friend… I've known him for a couple of years now and he's a really nice guy.' And the impressionist Alistair McGowan? 'He is someone who I really admire – I think he's such a talented man,' said

Jessie. 'I did meet him [on the night of the National TV Awards], but we were just chatting and that was the end of it. Then, suddenly, I'm meant to be going out with him!'

Then, in addition, there was that constant focus on all the other aspects of her life, as well. Jessie continued to learn the hard way that her off-screen activities were now lapped up by the public and almost certain to end up in the papers, while her alter ego – Kat – was meanwhile having a turbulent time of it in the Square. No storyline was too much for the nation's favourite East Ender and, by mid-2002, she was in the wars again.

This revolved around the Square's handsome Dr Trueman, and the unfortunate revelation that both Kat and her daughter Zoë looked on the good doctor with great favour. Not content with having the secret of Zoë's real parentage revealed, they had now become romantic rivals as well.

In essence, both of them went after Dr Anthony. 'There is going to be massive trouble ahead as mother and daughter go head-to-head for their man,' said an *EastEnders* insider. 'Anthony ended his brief flirtation with Zoë because of their twelve-year age difference. But he's absolutely mad with himself. And when he finds out she is going on a date with Jamie Mitchell, he becomes insanely jealous.'

In best soap opera style, of course, he also found

himself mixed up with Kat. 'He finds himself responding in a very physical way when she makes a pass,' said the insider. However, Zoë, who had taken up again with Jamie, her first-ever lover, discovers that the man she really wants is Anthony. 'Inside, Anthony is tormented,' the source went on. 'He just wants Zoë for himself.' It was highly-charged stuff – and the viewers loved it.

Off screen, however, Jessie's new life continued to veer from one extreme to the other. One day, she seemed to be on her best behaviour; the next, she slipped up and gave the tabloids yet more fodder for pieces about the lifestyle of their new star. Jessie ended up in the headlines yet again when she was said to have told a pool player in Los Angeles to shove his cue 'up his arse'. She herself was not pleased when the story came out. 'That was totally innocent!' she said. 'Some guy was taking his shot at the pool table, and I was sitting at the end on a table with some friends, and his cue hit me on the head. So I tapped the end of it, and the bloke turned around and started shouting 'cos I ruined his shot. I just said, "Get over yourself," and that was the end of it. But unfortunately, there was someone in the bar who used to be in *EastEnders* watching the whole thing and, for some reason, they decided to go to the papers with this exaggerated story.' It was clearly wearing her down.

And then there were the stories that were downright lies. Now that she was, in a sense, public property, Jessie was also having to learn that sometimes the most ludicrous stories appeared, with no grounding at all in reality. And then there were other occasions when something minor occurred and was blown out of all proportion or exaggerated. It all goes back to the British attitude towards celebrity – and the fact that the nation is so desperate for gossip that it will devour reports that simply aren't true.

'I've had to toughen up and learn to laugh at it, because it's the only way to deal with it,' Jessie said. 'It used to really upset me, especially reading stuff that wasn't true – I'd be in tears. But now I tell myself that it's just words and, as long as my family and friends know the truth, that's the most important thing.'

But the trouble was that now, as with the vast majority of celebrities, there were people who were actively trying to get Jessie to slip up. Some might have been journalists eager for a story, some might have been jealous rivals and some might just have wanted to make some money by tipping off a newspaper. But the fact was, they were out to cause trouble, and Jessie was just beginning to realise that.

'That happened at [the] Inside Soap Awards party last year,' she said in 2002. 'I didn't turn up until 10.30pm because I'd been working, and some journalist came up to me and asked me why I was so late, and was almost having a go at me. She was trying to make me retaliate to get a story out of it. It's like people are waiting for me to bite back, but I've learnt not to rise to it now. I went to a party a while ago and some girl literally pushed me off the dance floor – I ended up on all fours! I just stood up, brushed myself down, looked at her, smiled and walked away.'

This was quite a change from the fiery Jessie of her early career. Of course, underneath, her personality remained as dynamic as ever – and that showed, too – but she was having to learn patience and self-restraint. A successful acting career is not just about acting well, it is also about dealing with the accompanying fame. And for all the problems that Jessie encountered, she was beginning to build up reserves she hadn't known she possessed.

An essential piece of armour for anyone who wants to be famous over the longer term is resilience. It is, obviously, difficult to deal with all these pressures and the sensible celebrity will have an inner life that remains relatively untouched by their external status. This requires the ability to laugh off untruths, ignore provocation and, sometimes, exercise patience. It requires the ability to separate fact from fiction, not get too upset by either of them and remember that the advantages of such a life far outweigh the disadvantages – after all, the opportunities now open to Jessie were greater than anything she had ever dreamed of before.

And to make the most of those opportunities, she would have to cope with a level of pressure that most people simply cannot imagine.

She was learning, of course, but she still made mistakes. And it wasn't just Jessie who was occasionally in trouble, either. She might have had the highest profile of the relatively new arrivals in *EastEnders*, but she wasn't the only person who went from complete obscurity to nationwide fame almost overnight; another cast member was dealing with the same situation as well.

The youngest of the Slater family was Michelle Ryan, who played Zoë. At least everyone else was an adult; Michelle was just fifteen when she was chosen for the role, although she was well aware of what could happen to child stars. When she got the part, she announced, 'I've read about young stars who face problems and can understand how they get into trouble.'

It was a very sensible and grounded attitude. But, as with Jessie, all the warnings in the world won't prepare you for what it will really be like. And Michelle, while still very young, had as much pressure to deal with as anyone, and it came from several different directions. For a start, she had to cope with the demands of the various traumatic Kat/Zoë storylines. These were emotionally draining and would have taken it out of anyone, let alone someone who was still a young girl.

And then, like Jessie, there was the issue of overnight

fame. At least Jessie was an adult when it happened, with a background in which drifting had turned into a determination to succeed. Michelle, however, was little more than a child. She didn't have the reserves of experience that the others had to call upon, which made it doubly difficult to know how to respond to what was happening to her. Everyone around her was aware of this, and tried as much as they could to shield her from the more difficult aspects of being a star.

Despite the utmost efforts to keep her calm, however, Michelle's worried parents were forced to call the police when she went missing after the end of a relationship with *Hollyoaks* actor Gary Lucy, which led to *EastEnders* bosses giving her some time off. She recovered fully, but again, it was a telling episode. It really is not always easy being famous.

And even that had a knock-on effect where Jessie was concerned. Michelle's absence meant that storylines involving the two of them had to be put on the back boiler, which, in turn, meant that Jessie was not on screen as much as she had been in the past. This led to inevitable speculation that she was not happy with the way her on-screen life was moving. She had hit the ground running as far as the show was concerned, sweeping the popularity stakes and piling up numerous awards for her acting. Now, it seemed as if she was forced slightly on to the back foot.

Indeed, it was Kacey Ainsworth, who played the youngest of the Slater sisters, Little Mo, who seemed to benefit from all this. She began pulling in awards for her work hand over fist. Confounding the sceptics, Jessie was extremely generous about this. 'I am really thrilled about Kacey's success,' she said. 'And I think she is a brilliant actress. But I am just dying to get back in the spotlight again.' It was absolutely the right tack to take – gracious, while enthusiastic about what the future holds.

Indeed, Jessie was greatly relieved when Michelle returned to the show, and was hopeful that the two of them could have a calmer on-screen relationship – although she did acknowledge that was not necessarily very likely. 'I don't suppose the writers will – but I hope they make something good come between Kat and Zoë, and they get together again, I really do,' she said. 'I do like getting my teeth into good storylines. I have a special place in my heart for Michelle, and she brings out my mothering instinct in real life, too.'

It was, actually, quite interesting to compare the experiences the two actresses had. Despite the age difference, they were in almost identical positions, and both were learning how to cope as they went along. 'Yes, I've had to grow up quickly,' said Michelle. 'It's not just that the job's really responsible and hard work, it's all the pressures of fame. I'm not complaining – the advantages far outweigh the disadvantages – but you definitely pay a price. It's totally mad and sometimes it's hard to deal with.' That was exactly what Jessie had felt from the day it had all begun.

Like Jessie, Michelle tried to retain some semblance of a normal life, but it wasn't always easy. 'Even though I often stick my hair in a cap when I go out, I'm still recognised,' she said. 'That can be great, but it's also spooky. I'll go into a shop and a week later one of my friends will say, "So-and-so saw you in the supermarket and said you were buying such-and-such… "I'm scrutinised over everything. I'll be in a restaurant and suddenly I'll realise the table next to me has gone deadly quiet and everyone is listening to my conversation.

'Mum and I went to the Party in the Park in London this summer. Suddenly, everyone wanted my autograph. Mum got really scared for me because I was getting mobbed. We couldn't stay. She literally had to drag me through the crowd. I've had guys writing, asking for naked pictures or wanting to marry me. It's quite mad. And I've had crank calls on my mobile. However often I change the number, people still find it out. Blokes leave silly messages saying, "Is that Zoë's phone?" I also get people knocking on my door just to say, "Oh, that's where she lives."'

This was the kind of existence that could make anyone rather tetchy; all in all, Michelle was handling it remarkably well. And like Jessie, she had the problem of dealing with people who thought they were talking to the character she played, rather than the real person underneath. 'Lots of guys think I'm going to be like Zoë, whereas we're totally different – that's part of the fun of playing her,' she says. 'Guys often get too forward. I've had them come up and say, "Let's have a kiss." I don't want to be stand-offish, but it makes me cross. I'm not a little toy to be used. If I met the right person, I'd go out with him. But it's harder to trust guys now and that's a problem.' It sounded remarkably like the experiences of her older colleague and friend.

Of course, it was helpful for Jessie and Michelle to be able to compare their experiences. And, in some ways, Jessie seemed to be getting along quite well herself. Her growing wealth meant that she could afford a nice place to live, and so she sold her flat in Epping and bought a £600,000 house in East London, which she moved into with Bailey. 'I love it,' she said. 'I don't want to seem flash, but I got a good deal. It's a bit minimalist now because I've just moved in. I'll build it up by going to antique shops for art deco – I'm the chandelier queen!'

It was a good investment. It gave her a refuge and somewhere to retreat to when times got too tough, to say nothing of the fact that owning a London property, over the longer term, at least, is very frequently a good bet. It was also a sign of her growing success, not least because she had started to have problems where she had been living before.

'I was under pressure living in Essex and had people banging on my door in the early hours,' she said. 'At the end of the day, I'm just a normal girl who is an actress and I just want to get on with my job. I really hope I can shake off the image of my character at some stage in the future. I need the chance to be Jessie, not Kat.'

Another indication of her growing status within showbusiness circles was the fact that she was also now being invited to the great and good events in the showbusiness calendar, in this case Children in Need. She and a group of fellow *EastEnders* cast members took part in the twenty-third telethon for this most excellent of causes, and what they chose to do wasn't easy – they recreated Michael Jackson's famous video, 'Thriller'.

'Michael Jackson is a musical legend and a complete idol of mine,' said Mohammed George, who played Albert Square's Gus and was one of those taking part. 'I just hope I can remember how to moonwalk.' This is a sign that people are really being taken seriously by the Establishment – when they are allowed to participate in the great prime-time set pieces on TV.

Jessie was being appreciated in other quarters, too. There was yet another award to add to an already groaning windowsill, when she went home with the soap category in the Mental Health Media Awards, in recognition of the way she had played Kat, and challenging the stigma and silence that surround childhood sex abuse and suicide. This was a real acknowledgement of how far she had come; it was not a case of the acting community congratulating itself, as sometimes happens, but a serious organisation rewarding her for the work she had done. It was also a further indication that, one day, she would be able to take on much more serious roles than that of Kat, and had the ability to appear in a great deal more than *EastEnders*. The BBC looks out for signs like these; Jessie's latest triumph was sure to have been noted.

As yet, she had not got a serious new boyfriend. She was able to laugh at her single status, too, saying she fancied the actor Jamie Craven so much that she stuck a picture of him on her wall. 'He played Billy's big brother in the film *Billy Elliot* and he's gorgeous,' she said. 'I don't know him, but I've taken his picture out of a magazine and stuck it in my dressing room.' She was proving herself just an ordinary girl next door again – and her fans lapped it up.

Like so many women, she continued to be aware, at least, that she was hoping someone special would turn up. Jessie was still a young woman, but even so, work and social life were not absolutely everything. She got plenty of attention, too, and was constantly cited as one of the most desirable women on television. And yet, for now, that special someone continued to elude her grasp.

That she could cope with. But the confusion between Jessie and Kat consistently irritated her. There was some more slightly unfortunate publicity when she was pictured on holiday topless, most certainly not a heinous crime in itself, but it gave rise to yet another newspaper cutting of the kind Jessie could do without. She took it on the chin. 'Well, while I'm not saying I asked for it, I think I was a bit careless walking around without a top on,' she said. 'I should know by now that pictures like that are going to end up in the papers, so I do feel like it was my own fault. But I did find it annoying because it upset my mum.'

But she became resigned to it, just as she was to everything else. Like many well-known people, however, she was also having to accept that her family could be affected by what she did as well. 'I was worried for my mum and that my dad would see,' she said. 'But at the end of the day, I was looking for trouble. It's just one of those things. Someone I knew said, "You looked a bit rough in the papers with your baps out! But Elvis looked good." I've got an Elvis tattoo on my leg!' Her sense of humour was still functioning – Jessie was still able to recognise the ridiculous when she saw it, no matter how stressful other areas of her life might have been.

Yet again, though, she felt, with some justice, that she was attracting an unfair amount of attention because people associated her so strongly with Kat. 'People think I'm down the pub every night, but I'm quite a homely person,' she said, this time sounding both resigned and despairing of her lot. 'I like having friends over to my house, and I only go out once in a blue moon. And when I'm out, I'm just like anyone else in the pub.

'I've never pretended to be a goody two-shoes, but I'm not the devil the media has portrayed me as either. I've made some mistakes along the way and I have to learn the hard way. Because I play a character like Kat, people expect me to be like that in real life, and anything I do or say is totally blown out of proportion.' There was a great deal of truth to this, given the British public's ambivalence towards celebrity – but it was a price that Jessie ultimately felt was worth it. It's just that it could be hard.

And even the most casual and innocent of actions ended up on the front pages. On one occasion, Jessie did what literally millions of Britons do every day, and wound up in the papers because of that, too. 'I was pictured in my pyjamas recently, when I went outside to move my car,' she said. 'You really don't need someone sitting in front of your house, waiting to take a picture of you at 8.30am. When I saw those photos, I was gutted – I looked like a Tweenie!'

Again, the public lapped it up. Jessie was one of them. However, it was still felt in some quarters that she was just getting into the papers too much, and for all the wrong reasons. Reports of her lively behaviour might have been exaggerated beyond her or anyone else's control, but they were still out there and the BBC didn't like it.

Even so, no one foresaw what would happen next. Jessie was aware of the need to calm down and, on the whole, was trying to do so, because she was aware of how much her bosses disliked what they saw and read. Indeed, she had been warned several times by *EastEnders* bosses that she had to get her life under control, something, for whatever reason, she had been unable to do. But she kept trying to turn over a new leaf.

Under these circumstances, what happened next could not have come at a worse possible moment. Jessie was in the wrong, certainly, but did not foresee or expect the consequences of what she was doing. As far as the BBC was concerned, however, it was the straw that broke the camel's back.

In short, Jessie was charged with drink-driving. She had been apprehended in her Mercedes, allegedly one-and-a-half times over the limit, was arrested and given a court date. And for the BBC, that was just too much.

And so, in a move that shocked Jessie, her colleagues and fans, the powers that be in Albert Square took a drastic move. She was suspended from *EastEnders* at the end of 2002 for two months on no pay. They were most certainly not dropping her, but it was now felt that only firm action would bring the message home about how much she had to lose if she didn't pull herself together.

And it did the trick. From following a rather self-destructive path, Jessie was given the shock of her life and a clear pointer as to what would happen if she didn't get her act together. She had come so far – it would be madness to let everything she had worked so hard for slip away. And so she resolved that she would curb her wilder ways and be, if not a model employee, at least a fairly well-behaved one. The situation was clear – sink or swim. And Jessie, to the great relief of everyone around her, swam.

7

A New Leaf

In retrospect, being suspended from *EastEnders* was probably the best thing that could have happened to Jessie, because it brought her up sharp before it was too late. There is a long list of celebrities who have been ruined by instant stardom; in Jessie's case, having the threat of celebrity being removed, without it actually happening, was a massive shock, but one from which she could recover. Jessie was really very lucky – Elaine Lordan, who played Lynne Hobbs, did actually lose her job, whereas this was just a warning shot fired from some distance and, at this stage, did not prove fatal. But all the same, it felt to Jessie as though her world was falling apart.

And so, she took immediate action to start trying to turn around her public image, and resolved to address her wayward behaviour. She admitted later that she initially spent some time wallowing in depression, but she did not go under. Instead, she began making plans to present herself in a new light. Eager to distance herself from past antics, a very penitent Jessie attended the *TV Quick* Awards ceremony, at which *EastEnders* won five trophies. At the after-show party at the Dorchester, she was clearly beginning to realise what she'd done. She was completely open about it, blamed no one but herself and, in many ways, came across very well. Her bosses at *EastEnders* were left in no doubt as to how bad she felt.

She was also open about the constant pressure that she was now under, commenting on the fact that so many people tended to confuse the identity of Jessie and Kat and that she was so often expected to behave like her alter ego. She was adamant she was Jessie, not Kat – she didn't want to become embroiled in rows, she didn't want to cause controversies and she certainly didn't want to stop appearing in *EastEnders*. She was well aware now that something had to change.

'This year has been the worst of my life,' Jessie said. 'I just feel like everything I've achieved has been ruined. I can't go anywhere nowadays without people thinking that I'm really Kat. I'm expected to get into scraps and cause trouble but, at the end of the day, I'm just not like that. My life is being lived through the papers and I don't think I realised just what was going to happen when I joined the show. I'm just really not happy about anything at the moment and it's depressing to be in this sort of position.'

Depressing, yes, but the situation was not irredeemable, for the simple fact was that the BBC did not want to lose their rising new star. They did, however, want to impress upon Jessie just what was and was not a wise way to behave. So much had happened to her over the last few years that she had never really had a chance to sit back and consider the wider implications of her behaviour and her life, and that was what she was able to do now. She might have preferred to learn the lesson another way, but it was a salutary one, nonetheless.

Jessie genuinely was trying to make amends and she continued to be prepared to talk about it, too. The reason for the suspension gradually came out and, while she couldn't go into too much detail – there was, after all, a court case pending – she did not try to pretend that none of this had ever happened. 'A lot of things have happened in the past that placed me in breach of contract – like turning up late for work and things that happened away from work, which had an effect on the programme – and that's what led to the suspension,' said a gloomy Jessie afterwards. 'I can't go into it all, but it meant being off for two months.'

It was a very beneficial experience – tough love on

the part of the *EastEnders* producers, if you like. It showed Jessie quite how far she'd come and quite how much she'd got to lose if she messed up now – and it was a lot. She might have resented the constant attention, the intrusion into her personal life and the way people confused the personalities of Jessie and Kat, but worse, far worse, would be to have it all taken away again. One of the secrets of success in life is knowing when something is very much worth preserving, and that was certainly the case with Jessie's role on *EastEnders*. After all, it could lead to even greater things.

Again, she was very open about it all. 'The minute I found out I was suspended, I cried… I was really in shock,' she said. 'For the first month, I sat at home watching bad daytime telly and eating chocolate. My friends had to lift me off my arse and get me out of the house. It was really hard, I was moping around the house all day. I got into a bit of a hole, I was really down.'

She realised, though, that in many ways it was the wake-up call she needed. 'It was really hard, because not only was I away from the job I love, but I wasn't getting paid for two months,' she said. 'It was a real shock to wake up at 5.30am and realise that I didn't have to go to work. I missed the people, the place – everything. It makes you realise how precious your job is, and how easily it can slip through your fingers. I've really learned from it and, hopefully, now that I'm back,

I can move on and just forget about what happened. And hopefully other people can, too.'

She was open, though, about the fact that she'd been concerned she would never be allowed to return. 'Yes, I was worried,' Jessie confessed. 'You get these insecure moments. But it's fine now.'

Indeed, it wasn't just the fame that had been jeopardised, it was her whole way of life. Jessie loved being an actress and wanted to continue to be one, whatever role she eventually played. Had she not been allowed back, it would have sent out the message to other potential employers that she might be a bit difficult to handle.

And then there was the fact that, like any workplace in any profession, her colleagues made up a huge part of her life. Most people's work places become a home from home, a community in which you belong and in which you feel at home. Deprived of that, Jessie felt all at sea. Work often becomes a support, a lifestyle, sometimes even a refuge from the vicissitudes of life. It takes the place of the old village square in which people used to gather and gossip. Take a person out of that community for a while, and the sense of loss will be acute.

But it was good for her, and her friends agreed that this had been a warning in the nick of time. 'It was sort-your-life-out time for Jessie,' said one. 'She realised that she'd jeopardised a fantastic job that was beyond her wildest dreams. She realised that, in her position, you can't just go out and make a fool of yourself – people will notice, photographs will be taken and the powers that be at the BBC will not be happy.'

Jessie had certainly taken this lesson on board. Indeed, she was also keen to emphasise how well she got on with her fellow cast members, not least as there had been dark rumours about tensions on set, too. 'I'd say I get on well with a few people on set… it is really friendly,' she said. 'I'm close to the Slater family – particularly Laila Morse and Michelle Ryan. I love Chris Parker [Spencer Moon] to bits, and I really love working closely with Shane Richie [Alfie Moon]. We clicked straight away.

'Shane's a brilliant bloke, and Alfie's a fantastic character – him and Kat work so well together. There's a lot coming up where Alfie's trying to tell Kat how he feels and someone interrupts and it doesn't quite happen, and I reckon viewers will enjoy that. It's the start of a really good "Will they, won't they?" storyline.' It was interesting – Jessie was beginning to judge storylines not just as they came across to her, but in terms of what effect they would have on the viewer. She had clearly been picking up the tricks of her trade faster than ever.

And what, she was asked, about Jack Ryder? Jack, who played Jamie Mitchell, had alleged that there were tensions between the people who played the Slater family and everyone else on set. Jessie was having none of it. 'I never worked much with Jack, so I don't know why he said what he did, and I can't imagine why he said bad things about the show that made him,' said Jessie, who was clearly learning a thing or two about diplomacy and turning awkward allegations on their head. 'Maybe he thinks that's what people want to hear. But… I wish him all the luck in the world!'

And with that, it was back to business as usual. Jessie had been playing Kat for a couple of years now, and was clearly beginning to think of her almost as a friend. She had a great affection for the role she played, which came across on screen, both investing Kat with a real warmth and making her more real to the viewers. And Jessie was enormously relieved to be back playing the character she had brought so successfully to life; she could hardly stop talking about her.

'I love Kat,' she said. 'She's suffered so much. She wears a shell round her. Her thick make-up is like a mask that she wears. Since she met Alfie, she's almost become like a child again. I think Kat and Alfie were made for each other! The make-up's getting thicker and the skirts are getting shorter. I love going to work, putting the leopardskin on, the heels, the lip gloss, the chokers.'

In fact, she was even beginning to relish Kat's over-the-top style. 'I love it,' she said. 'The tackier the better!

I do my own make-up – I smack it on! When I'm driving home, I look in the mirror and think, "My God! I look like a transvestite!" People send me fake tan cream, lipsticks, there's even nail varnish named after Kat! Barbara Windsor bought me a bottle from the place where she gets her nails done.' If proof were needed that Kat had become a style icon, this was surely it.

And she tried even harder to distance herself from the recent past. The notorious picture of Elaine Lordan and Jessie emerging the worse for wear from a nightclub continued to surface. Jessie, however, was getting exasperated. After all, the photos had been taken some years previously. 'People just assume I'm a wild nightclubber, but I'm not,' she said. 'I go out once in a while, but the same pictures of me are used over and over again, like the one of me and Elaine when we first joined the show. We were coming out of a club a bit drunk and were going, "Wooh," and lifting our legs up and dancing down the street.' It had been a pretty innocent incident, but set a precedent and Jessie obviously didn't want to be reminded of it yet again.

She was also consistently supportive of her fellow stars. 'I love Laila Morse, who plays Mo; I love Chris Parker, who plays Spencer,' she said. 'He's gorgeous. I love Shane and the Slaters; it's a really nice environment.' Indeed, she got on with Shane particularly well. 'He's such a lovely bloke,' said Jessie. 'I didn't do any scenes with him before, but all the producers knew that Kat and Alfie were going to work. The chemistry is great. People ask me, "What's happening between Kat and Alfie?" and I say, "Oh, wait and see." Then they say, "And what's happening between you and Shane?" and I say, "Nothing! We just click."'

And she continued to impress. It seemed that with every awards ceremony that came round, Jessie got yet another gong, as the television industry acknowledged her growing talent. 'I've got eight in my cabinet at home – I've actually won twelve, but I haven't received four of them, all from a certain newspaper column that I won't name!' said Jessie 'I've been so lucky. Despite how difficult the last year was for me, I'm also aware how fortunate I am to get things like awards – it's been such a buzz. There isn't a single day that goes by when I don't look at them and feel so proud and so lucky to be where I am.'

Jessie, now that she was back on the show, was determined not to put her future at risk again. Asked how long she planned to stay on *EastEnders*, she replied, 'As long as the characters are fresh – and as long as they want me! I'd love to stay… look at Pat Butcher – her character has been through a million things but there are so many layers to her. They keep finding new storylines. I watched it from the very first episode. I've always loved Dot – I love June Brown, she makes me laugh. She's quite well spoken in real life. So is Pam St Clement. I try to be well spoken sometimes, but I slip back into Cockney!'

And once back in front of the cameras, she was quickly re-established as one of the prime interests on the show. For a start, she was pictured on holiday in the Caribbean island of Antigua, prompting much admiring comment from fellow holidaymakers. 'She didn't have all the make-up she wears on *EastEnders*, but you couldn't miss her,' said one. 'To start with, she was wearing a sarong over her bikini. That came off and you could see this Elvis tattoo, right on the front of her thigh.'

In fact, her holiday in Antigua proved to be more eventful than just a few weeks of rest. It prompted a holiday fling which, very briefly, looked as if it might become a long-runner. Ultimately, it didn't, but it did provide a bit of light relief at the end of what had been a trying couple of months.

Jessie was staying at the very upmarket St James Club in Antigua when she met Andy Burton, an American from Savannah, Georgia, who was in charge of the resort's water sports centre. There would appear to have been a very strong mutual attraction at first sight and the man himself was happy to furnish details of how they had first become an item. Initially, of course, he had no idea who Jessie was, but appeared to be delighted when he discovered he was romancing a big star.

'I still remember the first moment I laid eyes on her,' said Andy, after the romance had come to an end. 'I was walking past the pool where she was swimming and she shouted, "Oi, get me a coconut, will ya?" I'm quite a shy guy and would never have started talking to her unless she made the first move. I got her the coconut and laughed at her cheek. I thought she had a really pretty face and a great smile, but what really attracted me was her personality. She was really warm and happy. Jessie told me she was an actress, but I had never heard of *EastEnders* and certainly never heard of her.'

But something had clicked and the relationship began to blossom. The pair agreed to meet that night with their friends in The English Harbour, an elegant cluster of bars and restaurants, where they continued to get to know each other. They went their separate ways, but met up again the next day to go snorkelling. It was Jessie who then took matters into her own hands. She turned to Andy and asked, 'Why don't you kiss me?' Andy didn't immediately take her at her word. 'I suppose I was embarrassed,' he said. 'There were people around us and she was being so forward. I laughed and changed the subject.'

It was not long, however, before Andy took Jessie up on it, but, the course of true love never running smooth, she had to fly back to Britain the next day. She was clearly smitten, however and, after nine days of transatlantic phone calls, Jessie managed to take advantage of a break in the *EastEnders'* filming schedule and returned to Antigua to see Andy again.

This time she stayed with him and the two were clearly an item. It was an idyllic time – lots of swimming, sightseeing and lazing around – and they were able to take in the beauty of the island together. 'One evening, I took the boat out to show Jessie the sunset,' said Andy. 'She said how unfair it was that we lived so far apart. She said she had fallen for me in a big way. She knew I felt the same. It was then that I said I would consider moving to England to be with her. She didn't believe me – she wouldn't believe that I would give all this up just for her – but I would have.'

The boat, a fifty-foot black Seafarer that rejoiced in the name of *The Medallion*, had a black mast, two gold stripes down its hull and its name in gold lettering. A friend of Andy's was the captain and the locals were not surprised by the relationship. 'Andy has a way with the ladies,' said a barman at the St James Club's Casino bar. 'He likes to show them a good time.'

Another guest of the hotel, who had recognised Jessie, was fascinated by all the goings on. 'I saw them at the Docksider Ocean View Grill,' he said. 'They were watching a steel band and a fire-eater. You can't miss Jessie – she looked really sexy in this black, off-the-shoulder number. She kept stroking her boyfriend's arm while he caressed her face. She couldn't keep her hands off him. I couldn't believe it was Kat Slater, but there she was in a black bikini and a sarong.'

Andy claimed, however – and it was a claim he was happy to make in a newspaper after the relationship had run its very brief course, and so perhaps should not be taken too seriously – that Jessie was rather pleased when the photographers eventually and inevitably turned up. 'She would pretend she hated it and try to get away, but she really enjoyed the attention,' he said. 'I had the distinct feeling that she liked being snapped with me and even wondered if someone had tipped them off where we'd be – perhaps Jessie herself?'

Jessie soon had to return to the UK to continue filming *EastEnders*, but Andy followed her and spent a week on her home turf. 'I bought my flight ticket,' he explained. 'It was expensive, but worth it. At Heathrow, a buddy of mine picked me up and dropped me off at the BBC. I met some of Jessie's colleagues, but I couldn't tell you any of their names. She said they were quite famous.'

Andy stayed at Jessie's house, while she took him around town, including to the Cutty Sark in Greenwich and the Maritime Museum, pandering to Andy's passion for sailing. 'That was really thoughtful of her,' said Andy. 'She knew that I was hooked on boats, so it was the perfect day for me. We had a great week. We couldn't keep our hands off each other for one thing, but we also loved each other's company. She introduced me to her aunt and uncle, and had a few dinner parties so I could meet her friends. I thought we were the real thing.'

Jessie, alas, didn't agree. A relationship between an up-and-coming actress with a big future in Britain and an American, who lived in Antigua and was addicted to water sports, was never going to go the distance and so, shortly after Andy went home, Jessie rang and told him it was over. Andy was not pleased. 'She asked me, "How is this ever going to work?"' he said. 'She said the distance was too far. I was already planning to move to London. But she didn't want to see me again. I feel cheated. I invested a lot of feeling in our relationship, yet she threw it back in my face. I loved her and it's going to take a long time to get her out of my system. I was ready to give up everything and move to England for her. Then she ended it all.'

There was another reason for this, one that Andy forgot to mention – he had sold details of the fling to a magazine. He was also acting as if the relationship was far more serious than it really was. 'I wouldn't say an engagement or marriage is on the horizon, but we are going steady,' he said on his return from London. 'I stayed with her for a week. I am hopeful she will come here very soon when she gets time off work. You know, we just sort of hit it off. I had a great time in London.'

When Jessie found out what he had said, she was horrified and ended the relationship immediately. It's also true to say that Andy's behaviour didn't exactly restore her faith in men. 'Jessie was learning the hard way that when you're the best-known star in the nation's most popular soap opera, it can be very difficult to guard your privacy,' said a friend. 'She's been hurt like this so often that the poor girl's become almost obsessive about keeping her private life private.'

Openly, Jessie merely said, 'Yes, we have split. There were just too many miles between us, unfortunately.' In private, she was more forthcoming. 'I was shocked and disappointed, frankly,' she said. 'I can't go out with someone who is going to talk to all and sundry about our relationship.'

It had been a fling that had worked both ways. On the one hand, it had provided a couple of months' entertainment for the two of them – but on the other, not for the last time, Jessie had to put up with someone selling stories about her. It was hardly surprising that she sometimes found it hard to trust would-be suitors when she'd had a couple who had tried to profit directly from their time with her.

And there was a very nasty hangover from this visit that had not yet been made public. Jessie had indeed introduced Andy to her aunt and uncle – and had been arrested for driving over the limit when she was making her way home. But the repercussions of this were a little way off yet. It was, however, unfortunate, to say the least, given how Jessie had been making a conscious effort to play by the rules and show everyone that she was a reformed character.

Back on the set, however, all was running smoothly. And, once again proving that her fan base was a wide one, Jessie – or rather, Kat – then received a very different accolade. Kat Slater was voted the best screen mother by children in a survey carried out by the Internet firm AOL, beating Marge Simpson and Mrs Weasley (Ron's mother in the 'Harry Potter' films) into second and third place.

'We were surprised she came top,' said an AOL spokeswoman. 'But she is loving, loyal and cool. Kat fitted the bill better than more traditional mums like Marge Simpson or Mrs Weasley.' Becky Chatterley, twelve, was one of those who had voted for Kat. 'She doesn't let anybody mess with her or Zoë,' she said. 'She is the person we would all like to call Mum.'

The situation was rapidly calming down and now that past events were firmly in the past, other people were also beginning to reassess what happened. One of these was Hannah Waterman. On returning to the soap, Jessie had said that the two 'now get on'.

Hannah had a slightly different perspective,

however. 'Me and Jessie best mates? Er… no… never.' This was a personal argument which, unfortunately, has gone on and on. The reality is that working at *EastEnders* is no different to any office environment. You can never get on with everybody 100 per cent of the time. That said, the *EastEnders'* set is actually more like being at school than in an office. Hannah did concede, though, that her relationship with Jessie was not affecting their work. 'It's irrelevant to our daily lives these days,' she said, 'I'm just so embarrassed about what happened.' There was never going to be any love lost between the two of them, but at least they could work together. And both clearly wanted to forget the immediate past.

Having managed to keep her work life on a relatively even keel for a while, Jessie had yet another potential disaster to confront – it was eventually time for her drink-driving case to come before the courts. Despite all her attempts to retreat from the public gaze, and to simply get on with her work, she was unceremoniously thrust back into the spotlight with a vengeance.

Jessie was still felt deeply hurt by Andy Burton and had no further thought of another boyfriend, for now at least. She wanted to keep her head down, concentrate on her job and build up even more accolades for the role of Kat than she had already achieved; she wanted to continue to work in her dream job, and get the court case over as quickly as possible. But her court appearance was bound to attract onlookers and unwanted attention, and to help her through this, Jessie was assigned a policeman to look after her throughout the trial. His name? Dave Morgan.

8

The Long Arms of the Law

It was the talk of showbusiness circles. Jessie Wallace had a new boyfriend and the world wanted to know more. And that boyfriend, the twenty-eight-year-old policeman assigned to look after her during her court case, was clearly utterly besotted. Since her break up from Paul, Jessie had had a few flings, but nothing serious. Could she finally have met Mr Right? For a while it certainly seemed so, and the timing was right, too. Jessie was getting to an age when people start to think about settling down, and she had already admitted to feelings of broodiness. And it didn't hurt that she found her handsome policeman exceedingly attractive, too.

Dave Morgan himself was utterly enthralled by his new girlfriend, saying, 'She's my little cracker.' Her celebrity status, which might have alarmed some suitors, didn't worry him a bit; he seemed able to look beyond it to the real person on the other side. Neither was he put off by her flamboyant reputation, the constant press interest or the fact that he, too, would become a media target once linked with her. In May 2003, about a month after they first got together, he began to talk a little about the relationship that had taken everyone, the two participants included, by surprise.

'The moment I first set eyes on her, I was absolutely smitten,' he said. 'She's a gorgeous young woman. What man wouldn't be attracted to her? I think I made her feel at ease at a time when she was under a great deal of stress with the Court case and the photographers chasing her. I just cracked a few jokes with her and she seemed to really warm to me immediately.' She had indeed, and it was not long before the whole world knew about Jessie's new man.

The two had actually met on 22 April 2003. Dave had been sent by his bosses at Chelmsford Police Station to the court where Jessie was appearing on drink-driving charges. In the court itself, she denied the charge and was bailed to appear there the following September. She emerged, very upset, and was whisked into Dave's Ford Mondeo police car. It was as if he was a modern version of a knight in armour, carrying her from danger in her hour of need.

'When Karen first got in the car, she was really freaked out,' he said, calling Jessie by her real name, like the rest of her friends and family. 'She wasn't hysterical, but she was extremely upset and she was close to tears. I just told her to relax, and said, "There are worse things going on in the world." She started to smile a bit and, by the end of the journey, which only lasted twenty minutes or so, she was laughing and looked far more relaxed.'

They had clearly made quite an impact on one another. Jessie also remembered the time they first met. 'He just came over and started talking to me,' she said. 'He looked after me… reassuring me, saying, "It's going to be fine." I started giggling like a stupid teenager! I just fell for him – and he fell for me. It proves that you never know what's around the corner, even when you very least expect it. It's mad!' It was certainly very unexpected. But no matter; the two were being quite dewy-eyed about one another and, given that all the world loves a lover, all the world was charmed.

Dave actually charmed her through the most effective of methods – he cheered Jessie up. 'He made me laugh,' she confessed, when asked what first drew her to him. 'I remember he came over and sat down next to me. He was wearing his police jacket and he couldn't put his hands in the pockets, 'cos the pockets go the other way round so the officers can't be seen with their hands in them. But he was trying to put his hands in them the wrong way. He made me laugh straight away.'

Matters progressed quickly from there. There was an instant spark between the two, so much so that Dave got Jessie to give him her number before he dropped her off. A couple of days later, he used it. 'I was a bit nervous making that call, because I was worried she'd laugh at me and say she wasn't serious about wanting to see me again,' he said. 'But Karen was fine and she said she was just as nervous as me, so when we first went out together, we were like kids on our first ever date. She told me she loves tall, dark men, so I'm happy she's gone for me.' The date was a resounding success.

And, again, it seemed as if Jessie really had met the man of her dreams. She might have said in the past that she only wanted a boyfriend in showbusiness, but Dave came across as being utterly dependable and a pleasant distraction from the cares of the showbiz lifestyle, which could sometimes feel too much for Jessie, even now.

And he fitted in with her lifestyle, too. Despite all the drama she was prone to encounter, Jessie had remained close to the people she knew before she had an acting career, and so Dave was meeting not just showbiz types but old friends from her past, too. And it all seemed to be going very well, the couple found out that they really did get on extremely well together.

In fact, their relationship naturally gathered momentum despite Jessie's concerns about the unreliability of men generally. She might have been a big star by this point, but big stars are as susceptible to human emotion as anyone else, and so it was proving to be with these two. It wasn't long before both were convinced that they had met their ideal soul mate.

But it did not take long before there was trouble in paradise. Jessie's knack for attracting controversy clearly spread to everyone she surrounded herself with and, in no time at all, Dave found himself at the centre of a newspaper report, which accused him of running off with his best friend's wife. It claimed that when Dave had been a fireman, as he had been before joining the police force, and as he was to become again, he had had a relationship with Sam Godfrey, a mother of three, who had been married for eight years to John Godfrey, his closest friend. The story, when it came out, caused a sensation, for while not famous himself, he had been touched with the gold dust of celebrity by association. And, as he learnt all too rapidly, that can have its ups, but also its downs.

Indeed, Dave was not thrilled about this early taste of life in the spotlight, and reacted angrily. That makes me bloody furious, because it's supposed to make me out to be some sort of love rat, which I'm not,' he said. 'There's more to that whole situation than meets the eye, but I'm not going to spread muck like others have. What makes me mad is that other people seem determined to ruin things for me and Karen, which is crazy. I've only just met her and it's early days for us.'

Of course Karen – or rather, Jessie – had grown used to this sort of treatment over the years. From the people who would try to goad her into making a scene in public, to the so-called friends who sold stories about her, to the jealous rivals who would try to do her down, she was well aware of the pitfalls that celebrity can bring. And given that she found herself at the centre of so many dramas, she would have been well aware that if someone had the means to cause trouble, then they would. Dave might not have been able to understand why the rest of the world wouldn't leave them in peace, but Jessie was getting used to it now. She had become a story – and so, therefore, was everyone close to her, too.

But Dave had never experienced it before and for him it was quite an eye-opener. He was also concerned about the impact this could have on his work. The police force, after all, could be forgiven for feeling that its officers should not be appearing in the newspapers every week, even if it is through no fault of their own. All that had happened was that Dave had found

Above: Jessie relaxes by spending time with one of her three dogs.

Below: Jessie with Shane Richie during an *EastEnders* shoot at Windsor Racecourse on 3 October 2005.

Jessie with the other *EastEnders* girls at The National Television Awards. From left: Kasey Ainsworth (Little Mo), Michelle Ryan (Zoë), Jessie (Kat), Lucy Benjamin (Lisa), Fansin Outhwaite (Melanie).

Above: Jessie and then boyfriend Dave take a horse carriage ride around Central Park while on holiday in New York.

Below: Jessie sits with her step-sister Danielle, a rising star in the modelling world.

Top left: Jessie with Michelle Ryan, who plays Zoë in *EastEnders*. The revelation that Zoë was Kat's daughter tackled the difficult subject of the sexual abuse of children.

Top right: Jessie partying at the Attica nightclub in London in 2001. Her wild lifestyle would land her in trouble with the BBC.

Below: Jessie and Shane Ritchie make a public appearance for The Princes Trust at Party In The Park in Hyde Park on 6 July 2003.

Top left: Jessie shortly before the birth of her daughter Tallulah Lilac.

Top right: Jessie at The British Soap Awards, where she won Best Newcomer and Sexiest Female.

Below left: Jessie with Shane Richie at the National Television Awards, 28 October 2003. She was awarded Most Popular Actress.

Below right: Jessie and then boyfriend Dave Morgan with newborn baby Tallulah Lilac.

Drama offscreen as Jessie and Dave Morgan leave Southend Court House, where Jessie was tried on drink-driving charges.

Jessie juggles the responsibility of motherhood with her love for fashion.

Now an independent single mother, Jessie has some big projects on the horizon.

himself a famous girlfriend, but now he was feeling the full heat of the media's interest, too. 'I know I haven't done anything wrong and none of this interferes with my job,' he said. 'But if people are out to make trouble for me, then that could be a problem with my bosses. But I want to carry on seeing Karen and she wants to see me.'

Initially, it seemed that that was not to be. Reports surfaced that the couple had split up, with Jessie saying, 'He's a really nice guy. The way we met and the media interest made it go off the boil, so we decided to call it a day.' But in reality that wasn't quite what had happened. What it seemed that they really decided to do was to say they'd call it a day, while actually continuing to see each other, in the hope of getting some privacy. Some hope!

Jessie was actually very pleased with the way her new relationship was going, and back at work all was also back on track. The events of the last year were fading from her memory, and her character remained as popular as ever. Indeed, she was having a lot of fun again, and was absolutely thrilled when George Michael visited the set of the show as a surprise fortieth birthday present arranged by his friends. Indeed, so thrilled was she, that she announced she'd like to go to bed with him. 'He's every woman's ideal man – if I could, I would,' she said.

George, who is gay, was unlikely to play along, but

Jessie did receive a big hug. 'He may be a devoted fan of *EastEnders*, but I've loved him since I was a girl,' she said. 'George was lovely, really friendly. It was surreal to meet him and I can't believe he thought the same.'

Indeed, the visit was a great success. Kenny Goss, George's boyfriend, had been behind it, along with his friend David Austen and his manager Andy Stephens. George spent time looking around the set, as well as meeting some of the other actors and actresses on the show. 'George has been a huge fan of the show for years,' said his spokesman. 'It was a brilliant birthday surprise and he had an amazing day.'

A spokeswoman from *EastEnders* was equally fulsome. 'George has been a life-long fan of *EastEnders* and knew everything about every character when he met them,' he said. 'He was fascinated to see how the programme was put together and said he had a fantastic time.'

And speculation about Kat's own future continued. She had, by now, become such a stalwart of the show that there was a great deal of talk about where she would go next. Would she stay on for decades and become a long-standing member of the cast? Would she go on to have children? Then, of course, there was the tricky matter of Jessie's own ambitions; the BBC was clearly grooming her for stardom, which meant that greener pastures still were a real possibility in the future. Jessie, very wisely, maintained a fairly neutral stance.

'I think having children might take the colour out of Kat, so I'm not sure [about that],' she said. 'I think there'll always be trouble for Kat and that's what adds to her character. As long as the character stays fresh, I'd love to stay in the show, but if it starts to go downhill then I think it would be time to move on. But at the moment it's really good.' It was a wise way of looking at it – and left every possibility open for the future.

Meanwhile, in the background, Jessie's relationship with Dave was going from strength to strength. She announced that it felt quite strange to go out with a policeman, 'because I'd never met a nice one before,' but, of course, it was Dave who was really having to cope with the strangeness of the situation. When most relationships begin, the couple involved have some privacy, but, in this case, it was being played out in the full glare of the public eye. It might be strange to become famous overnight, but it can be a little odd to absorb fame by proxy so suddenly, too.

Dave seemed to cope with it well. 'At the end of the day, it's Jessie's job,' he said. 'Admittedly, it was a bit strange to start off with, but really, she just goes and does her day's work the same as I go off and do mine. At first, there were a few of them [Dave's friends] who'd ask loads of questions. But I'm not the sort of person who goes around talking about it, really. I keep myself to myself.'

It didn't take long, though, before he started to be drawn further into Jessie's world. He'd had an early taste of it with the story about a friend's wife and he was beginning to discover that now that he was with Jessie, everything he did became news, too. As the two of them were increasingly pictured together, Dave even started getting recognised in his own right.

Jessie commented on the fact that he was soon asked for his autograph – 'That was weird,' said Dave – and, of course, people continued to fall over Jessie when they were together. 'Sometimes it can be strange when they shout, "Oi, Kat Slater!" when you're in the shopping centre or something,' he said. 'But at the end of the day, it's just part of Jessie's job.'

The relationship continued to develop quickly. Within a few short months, the two had not just become inseparable, but Dave had actually moved into her house. More than ever it appeared that Jessie had finally met her Mr Right, and that, during this honeymoon period, it seemed as if nothing could go wrong between them. They appeared to be getting closer every day.

The job was also going along extremely well. Her short break from the set of *EastEnders* did not mean Jessie was any less well regarded than before; she was voted the most popular actress at the National Television Awards. Her character, Kat, was proving to be more popular still. She was a real focal point in the programme, to the extent that even people who didn't watch *EastEnders* had heard of Kat Slater. But even Jessie herself was at a loss to explain Kat's appeal.

'It's hard for me to say, because I don't know what people see – all I can say is there are so many sides to the character,' she said. 'Recently, we've filmed these scenes where she's all loved up with Alfie and then she has a little run in with someone where she shrieks, "Whatchu looking at?" You know – one of those. And it's great because she's so loved up, then you think, "Please let her show the old Kat." That's what I love about the character – she can fly off the handle at any minute.'

The same might be said about Jessie, but she was adamant that those days were behind her. Instead, she and Dave lived a discreet domestic life together, enjoying themselves by dining out. 'I'm going out for dinner with my friends,' said Jessie. 'My favourite place is a restaurant in East London called Les Trois Garçons. I can't have dinner parties at the moment because my house is like a building site. I'm having bathrooms put in and getting it decorated, so I'm avoiding having people round. I've got someone doing it all and Dave's helping out. He lives with me in East London and we love it there.'

When she did go out in public, as it were, her

excursions were increasingly of the kind associated with the biggest names in showbusiness, rather than just a night at the pub. Dave went along on these occasions, too, of course, and, in retrospect, it's possible to see that ultimately this might cause a problem. For while Jessie's world had changed overnight when she started on *EastEnders*, that change did actually stem from the work she was doing and the new world she was being introduced to. Dave, on the other hand, was being introduced to that world purely because he was now Jessie's boyfriend. It made a difference and one that might turn out to be fraught with difficulties.

For now, at least, the couple were deliriously happy and revelling in their domesticity at home and the grand showbusiness occasions that both were now beginning to frequent.

Asked what the most spectacular of the lot was, Jessie replied, 'I think David Gest's fiftieth birthday party at the Dorchester, where Liza Minnelli sang. I was right at the front with Claire Sweeny… she's lovely. And I spoke to Joan – my friend Joan Collins! We had a little chat, she's so beautiful! I met Jane Russell and Petula Clarke there, too. It was such an experience; I thought 'I'm never going to see this again! I absolutely idolise Joan Collins and she's everything you expect. When she walks into the room, everyone just turns and she's got this fantastic aura. I'd love to be like that – I want to be Joan!' And who's to say that Jessie won't match some of Joan's accomplishments?

Indeed, work was going from strength to strength. Fellow *EastEnders* star Shane Ritchie was also enjoying a great deal of attention, and Jessie got on extremely well with him. 'He's very funny,' she said. 'We could be doing a really serious scene, looking into each other's eyes, and then suddenly there's this twinkle and that's it, we're completely thrown into a fit of giggles. We had some funny moments filming the wedding episodes, like this one moment when we were sitting down together and I was moving towards him and my dress was rubbing against the leather of the chair and it was like "paaaaaaaarp" and we just burst out laughing. I also had to do this thing where I nudge him in the stomach and I actually hit him in the goolies and he was trying to hold it together for so long before he screamed, "Aaaaargh!" and everyone started laughing. As soon as Shane walks on to the set, there's just laughter. It's really great.'

Another of Jessie's friends on the show was Nigel Harman, who played Dennis. As has already been revealed, he and Jessie went back a long way and she was thrilled to renew the acquaintanceship. Indeed, she was now in the position where she welcomed him to the show and was pleased at his growing reputation – quite a change from the days when she was backstage rather than in the spotlight. And as he grew in popularity, Jessie was characteristically generous about her old friend.

'Oh, he's gorgeous!' she said. 'I like the way Nigel says what he thinks. I knew him before. I used to do the wigs in *Mamma Mia!* and he was in that and I had to spray him down with water every night – naked from the waist up – oooh! It was great when he came into the show, and Dennis is a fantastic character. I'm so pleased Nigel won the most Popular Newcomer award.' That was an example of one of Jessie's qualities that is rarely written about – she has real charm and enormous warmth. It's hardly surprising she has built up such a loyal following over the years.

Shane was getting quite a few fans among *EastEnders'* female viewers and the admiration male viewers had for Jessie continued to grow. Jessie was as bemused by that as she was by Kat's popularity. 'I think it's the character… I don't think it's me!' she said. 'It's the costumes as well. If I were playing a humdrum character, I wouldn't get the awards. It's definitely the costumes, the lipstick and the make-up – and Kat's got this great tongue-in-cheek way about her. I love going into work and slapping on the make-up and the leopard- and tiger-print and then doing my mincing around the studio – I love it!'

Again, there was a constant pressure to look good.

Jessie did, without that much effort, but continuous comment in the press meant she had to stay on her toes. Jessie and her co-star Shane both had a go at the Atkins diet, but it didn't last. 'They've [the BBC canteen] actually got a protein bar in there now,' said Jessie. 'But the problem with being at work is the boredom when you're sitting around between scenes… you end up snacking on junk food and that's my downfall. If I smoked, it would be different, but I don't, so I'm thinking of getting a treadmill in my dressing room.'

This was quite a departure. For all the talk about short bursts of exercise, Jessie had never gone so far as talking about having equipment installed. More surprisingly still, she revealed that she already had one at home. 'Well, I've got a treadmill at home and I've been looking at it!' she said. 'And I've got a yoga DVD that I watch while eating a big cream cake! I've got dogs and so I walk them… I mean, when I get home, the last thing I want to do is go out jogging. And I have to be at work at 7.00am. I often set the alarm early and then it goes off and I just can't be bothered. I need motivation, I need someone to grab me by the hair, kick me out of bed and shout, "Go and get on it!"'

She was adamant, however, that she was under no pressure to lose weight. There had been some talk that the BBC wanted her to shed a few pounds, but Jessie point-blank denied this. 'No, they didn't ask me to do that – they wouldn't,' she said. 'And if they did, I'd probably laugh. There was a line that Kat was meant to say once, to one of my sisters in the show. It was, "You can never wear too much make-up and you can never be too skinny." I refused to say that line – you don't have to be slim to be attractive.'

She was absolutely right, but the fact remained that some papers still became highly critical if she looked as if she was carrying as much as a couple of extra pounds. Indeed, they were completely unforgiving, something that sometimes caused Jessie a great deal of pain. Asked if she minded when they had a go, she replied, 'Of course. It's so hurtful and horrible to be criticised for the way you look.

'There was a thing in the paper the other day saying that I looked fat in my *EastEnders*' wedding dress and that was spiteful, it really was. At the end of the day, I like to think I do a good job and I work really hard and then they criticise the way I look. I'm not a model, I'm an actress – I don't rate myself as anything else. The first thing I want to do [when I read these reports] is reach for the slimming tablets but then I think, "No! these people aren't going to make me ill." If you don't like the way I look, then sod you! I've got four awards in my cabinet for sexiest female, so it goes to show you don't have to be skinny to be sexy. If people have a problem with my weight, then that's purely their problem. At the end of the day, I'm a real woman and this is the way I am.'

Of course, Jessie's defiant attitude and her insistence that she maintained a curvy figure increased her popularity all the more. And, say what you like about Jessie and Kat, they were doing a good deal to redress the balance in recent years that dictate that any female star has to be painfully slim. For all her controversial behaviour, this was one area where Jessie was doing untold good. She hadn't asked to be a role model but, as Kat Slater, she was one, and she was turning into an excellent role model at that.

'I get loads of letters from young girls telling me how much they love Kat and that she's a great role model because she's proud of her body shape,' said Jessie. 'I don't think it would suit the character if I was thin. I was watching *Maid in Manhattan* the other day and I thought Jennifer Lopez looked beautiful in it. She has an hour-glass figure like Marilyn Monroe. If I was around in Marilyn's day, I would have been slated about my size like I am now, so it's not fair. Don't be hung up about weight. If you're happy, then don't change for anybody, only change for yourself.'

In fact, Jessie could be said to be the embodiment of a new type of emerging woman, who is the very antithesis of 'lollipop ladies' – the stick-thin actresses who resemble a lollipop because their heads are too big for their bodies. This new type includes J-Lo, of course, Nigella Lawson and Jessie herself. And for all the criticism she received because of her curves, Jessie had the constant reassurance of knowing that she was a bona fide sex symbol, no matter how much she continued to find her new status strange to come to terms with. If she was regularly cited as one of the most desirable women in the country, then that, more than anything else, showed her detractors quite how wrong they were.

Not that she wasn't averse to using every trick of the trade. She was becoming a wonderful spokesperson for anyone with a curvy figure, but even Jessie admitted that she might be tempted to go under the surgeon's knife or, even more daringly, have Botox. And why not? Legions of women have a little nip and tuck these days and it was refreshing that Jessie, at least, was open about it.

'I don't want it yet, but if I had a problem, I'd definitely have it done,' she said. 'I'd have my eyes done, a tummy tuck… the lot! I think, "Go for it. If that's what you want, then do it." I saw Debbie Harry the other day and she admits to having had it all done… she looks spectacular. And I thought, "Great… good for you." Why deny it?'

And, for all the constant pressure to keep up appearances, Jessie loved that side of life, too. Clothes and make-up are traditional female preoccupations, all the more so for an actress, and she revelled in both. 'Oh yeah, I love make-up; I used to be a make-up artist,' she said. 'I can't step out of the front door without foundation on at least. I spent God knows how much money on make-up and skincare products when I was in New York recently. I do my own make-up on the show, too, and I love applying the blues, greens and red lipsticks for Kat.'

And, of course, she adored clothes. Jessie was now a genuine style icon, her look was both photographed and copied and her fans were always keen to discover what she was to wear next. And this love of clothes was not a recent one. Jessie's grandmother had instilled it in her when she was a child, and it was a love that has lasted to this day. Her personal sense of style was also continuing to develop; it really was much classier than Kat's, much more elegant and much more striking. She was developing a real sense of how to put together a striking and sophisticated look.

Asked if she bought many clothes, she replied, 'Yeah, especially in vintage shops… I collect '40s clothes. I had quite a spree on my Visa in New York and bought some vintage handbags from the shop that the stylist for *Sex and the City* goes to. I adore hats, too. And I love autumn and winter because I can wear all my hats. I've got loads in autumnal colours, like rust greens and chocolate-brown.'

And so, all in all, life appeared to be going well. Jessie's popularity was growing by the day; she was developing into a consummate actress, one of the stars in the BBC pantheon and one commonly talked of as having a great future. She was feeling secure within herself, more settled than she had been for years and, in her relationship with Dave, seemed on the face of it to have met the man she was going to spend her life with. It appeared that everything was finally going her way.

But in the life of Jessie Wallace, nothing is ever that simple. Whether it's just chance, or whether she has the kind of personality which means she could summon up trouble if she was alone in a room, there was still a great deal more to come. For a start, that drink-drive charge was still hanging over her and she had yet to have her full day in court. Then there was the relationship with Dave, which did not continue quite as smoothly as it had started out. And, above all, of course, was Jessie's own persona – larger than life and with the ability to attract attention, whatever it was that she happened to be doing. Far from settling down, her rollercoaster life was to deliver some more stomach-churning twists and turns.

9

Drama Queen

Looking at it from the outside, it is sometimes tempting to think that being Jessie Wallace must be exhausting. No incident in her life is without drama. Just when she seems to have sailed serenely into calmer waters, a foaming wave inevitably threatens to engulf her and anyone associated with her. Late in 2003, the circumstances surrounding her private and public life followed this well-worn pattern. Yet more upheavals lay directly ahead.

For a start, as the relationship between Jessie and Dave progressed, not everyone, it seemed, appeared to be totally happy for the young couple. One such person was Georgina Davis, an office administrator from Billericay, Essex, who had previously been Dave's girlfriend. Livid that her boyfriend was now living with someone else, she couldn't help herself and launched into a tirade of abuse about Jessie just one week after she had won Most Popular Actress at the National Television Awards.

'If the viewers knew what she was really like, no one would ever watch her again,' Georgina said. 'When I heard that she had won that award, I just laughed my head off. It's not even as if she is good-looking. You only have to take one glance at her to realise that it's not her looks he's gone for. Sometimes you see her in the paper and she looks as ugly as sin. She's put on so much weight and looks like a beached whale.

'But if he thinks Jessie Wallace is more attractive than me, he's absolutely mad. That's what everyone tells me and they're right. He's only interested in her money and in using her as a passport to fame. She obviously doesn't care about anyone except herself – how else could she do this to another woman?'

It was clearly the massive upset of a woman scorned, albeit an upset that made the headlines, as everything in Jessie's life seemed to do these days. Georgina felt that Jessie had stolen Dave away from her, saying the two had been closely attached before she came along. And since Jessie was rich and famous, she felt that these two elements had been more of a motivating factor for Dave's feelings than they should have been.

Her hurt was understandable, although perhaps it should have been directed towards her ex rather than

Jessie. It was not Jessie who had gone after Dave, but vice versa; indeed, it is not clear whether she even knew that he had a girlfriend when the two of them met. And, if truth be told, Dave and Georgina had been together less than a year when Jessie came along. It was not as if she was trespassing into a long-established relationship. Even so, Georgina was clearly very hurt and it's no easier to lose a boyfriend to a celebrity sex symbol than to the girl who lives down the road.

'I thought Dave was going to be my husband,' Georgina said. 'He told me almost every day he wanted to marry me but, out of the blue, Jessie Wallace comes along and snatches him. She destroyed my plans for the future and my hopes of settling down with Dave. I don't know how she can live with herself. She's just a selfish cow and he's little better. They deserve each other.'

In fact, Georgina was adamant that there had been a complete change in Dave's personality since meeting Jessie in court. 'He came back that day really cocky,' she said. 'He seemed really pleased with himself for having met Jessie and for being on TV chaperoning her. From then on, everything changed. He started taking loads of care of his appearance and even joined a gym. He kept saying he had to go up to London to visit friends, but now I realise he was seeing her.'

Indeed, Georgina obviously believed her ex-boyfriend had become completely star struck. 'I think he was blinded by her fame,' she said. 'If it wasn't for the fact she's on *EastEnders*, he wouldn't look at her twice. I don't think she realises that. What he had with me was love – it was two soul mates together. That's not what Jessie Wallace is going to get.'

Dave had apparently behaved rather badly. Georgina only found out what was happening when she discovered Jessie's number on his telephone and was forced to ask who she was. 'I asked who Jessie was and the colour drained from his face,' said Georgina. 'He said it was just a friend at first, but then admitted it was her. We had a massive row before I stormed out.'

According to Georgina, that wasn't the end of their relationship. About a week later, he got in touch again. 'He phoned to tell me it was all a big mistake,' she said. 'He said he wanted to marry me and he would sort everything out. I went to his flat later in the week and we lay on his bed fully clothed, kissing and cuddling. He said he still loved me. But he told me I couldn't stay – he said it was because of the press. But I think it was because he didn't want Jessie to find out.'

Dave was clearly going to have to make a decision, and fast, and it was ultimately with Jessie that he saw his future panning out. And after seeing Jessie and Dave pictured together, poor Georgina realised her relationship with Dave really was over. 'It's been so hard because, everywhere I go, I see pictures of them together,' she said. 'It's like they were rubbing it in my face. The hardest point was when I saw photos of them in New York. We planned to go together but he took her instead. I also noticed he was still wearing a ring on his finger that I gave him for Christmas. It's engraved on the inside, "I love you". I wonder what Jessie Wallace thinks about that? If I were her, I wouldn't like it.'

Neither was she thrilled that Dave had now moved in with his new love. 'He's had his head turned by fame and money,' she said. 'He was always into labels and things and that's what he's interested in – her wages. I didn't have so much money to offer but I know I gave him more than she'll ever be able to. Jessie might have this glamorous lifestyle and all her money and cars, but none of that can buy you love. I think they're made for each other – neither of them will find happiness if they carry on this way. They'll end up two very lonely people.'

Indeed, once started, Georgina didn't really see any reason to hold back. 'She's as fickle with men as he is with women,' she said. 'I think she's just like Kat Slater – she's never going to find the right man. It doesn't matter that she's famous and rich – at the end of the day, she's the other woman. But now I realise it's the best thing that ever happened to me. She's more than welcome to him. And soon she will find out what he's all about. Jessie's going to have to live with him and that's punishment enough.

'I've got much more to offer than she does – to the people I care about, my friends and my family. She may be rich in cash, but I'm richer in life. I know how to be happy and to make other people happy. All that matters is that I'm shot of him. I had a lucky escape. In the end, Jessie Wallace did me a favour.'

Jessie responded, in public at least, with dignity. She said nothing. By now, well aware that there was nothing the media enjoyed more than watching her engaged in a row, she wisely rose above it. There was nothing to be gained from attacking a woman in pain, especially one who did not match Jessie's advantages in the shape of fame and wealth. But it was yet more publicity she could have done without.

It really was true – in every area of her life bar none, she made headlines. If meeting and falling for the policeman who escorted her from court was not unlikely enough, she even found herself condemned by the policeman's ex-girlfriend. If this had been a plot on a television soap opera, it would have been derided as sensationalist nonsense.

And, indeed, once the bandwagon started rolling, it was proving very difficult to stop. It seemed that neither Jessie nor Dave could do anything without provoking comment, and it was not long before Dave found himself to be the subject of yet more unwelcome headlines. It wasn't just Jessie who was scrutinised closely every time she did anything, it was Dave, too. And he seemed to have almost as effective a knack as Jessie for finding himself in the thick of it, as was shown when a case in which he was involved came up in front of an appeal judge and was thrown out of court, because of the way in which the police had handled the initial investigation.

The case involved a woman called Sharon Pharoah, who had been arrested after she arrived at her son's flat in South Woodham Ferrers, Essex. A group of policemen, including Dave, were already there on another matter when she arrived, and said that she shouted, swore and punched them. Dave arrested her and she was charged with assault, later being found guilty at Cheltenham Magistrates' Court. Sharon was ordered to do 150 hours' community service and pay £100 compensation.

But Sharon, who has a law degree, was quite adamant that she was completely innocent... and she had recorded some of the encounter on her mobile phone, which she brought to the next hearing. The court listened to it and heard her being co-operative, politely asking the police officers if they had a warrant. Her conviction was promptly overturned, and the people involved heavily condemned.

'A number of things that have been said by the officers simply cannot be right,' said the appeal judge,

Recorder David Turner. 'We have looked at the evidence as a whole and regret to say we have significant concerns about the credibility of a number of the prosecution witnesses.' Essex Police promptly launched an inquiry – 'We have received a complaint and it is under investigation,' a spokesman said.

This was all very embarrassing for Dave, not least because Sharon singled him out for criticism. 'When I see Morgan walking around with Jessie Wallace in the papers, it makes me so angry,' she said. 'He was so cocky and full of himself, he thought he could get away with anything. Morgan was a cocky little sod, who loved the fact he was in uniform. I told him I had a law degree and the arrest was out of order.'

Sharon was plainly steaming with anger, and she didn't stop there. She was absolutely determined to tell the world what had really happened and that she was furious about what happened, and especially Dave's part in it. 'He kept grinning,' she said. 'That's why I think they went ahead with it. They didn't like me standing up to them. At the trial, I called him "Pretty Boy" – he was really into being in the Police. He was the only officer who made eye contact with me in court. I want justice. The officers gave evidence which helped convict me of something I didn't do.'

It was all extremely unfortunate. About the only thing that could be said about it was that it was the kind of case that was unlikely to happen again, as Dave had already decided that he wanted to leave the police force and go back to being a fireman. Jessie announced the move with typical panache. 'He was a fireman for five years and he misses it,' she said. 'I'm pleased because I prefer the fireman's uniform!'

As ever, there was a good deal of speculation as to what really lay behind the move. Could anything in the world of Jessie and Dave ever be taken at face value? It seemed not. In the past Dave himself had spoken openly about not wanting to upset his bosses by the increasing amount of coverage that there was in the papers, and there were many onlookers who now believed he had done just that. He seemed to be pictured almost as much as Jessie, seemingly always in the thick of it, at a different club, party or show-business occasion every night.

And Dave himself had seen that something had to change. He had previously asked for a transfer from Chelmsford to Chigwell Traffic Police, to be closer to Jessie, but the request had been turned down.

'We can confirm that an officer has resigned from Essex Police for personal reasons,' said a spokesman. 'It would be improper to discuss reasons for his decision.' But there were plenty of others who didn't feel the need to hold back; there was intense speculation that with Jessie's drink-drive case looming, Dave would work as her driver, should she be banned from driving. Dave, like Jessie, was beginning to learn that life in the spotlight can be hard.

He was also having to put up with the same pressures as Jessie, but without the advantages. For all the problems she had to endure, Jessie was still a massively successful soap star, with a big salary, a nice house and a fantastic future. Dave only had this by proxy. He, too, was getting it in the neck every time he stuck a toe out of line, but he didn't have the resources Jessie had to fall back on. The two of them could be forgiven for wishing for a long period of peace and quiet.

But that was not, by a long shot, the end of their troubles. The next embarrassment occurred just days later, when it emerged that Jessie would not be able to attend her co-star Shane Richie's star-studded book launch at the Noble Rot for *Rags to Richie: The Story So Far*.

The reason, it seemed, was that another attendee was one Kevin Adams, a star of *Fame Academy*. It had been widely reported that he and Jessie had been snogging at a party at the Funky Buddha club after the National TV Awards, a claim Jessie strenuously denied, and yet which would not go away. It was alleged that Dave had gone out to the car for a snooze, while Jessie got a little carried away.

'The pair spent the night snogging and were literally the last to leave the club,' said one onlooker. 'There must have been words between her and Dave on the way home.' Another onlooker said that Jessie had been complaining that Dave didn't give her enough freedom. It was now said that Dave didn't want her to go to the launch because Kevin would be there, too.

'Dave still feels a bit awkward about everything that went on that night and, to be honest, Jessie didn't want to fan the flames,' said a friend. 'She swears the incident with Kevin was totally innocent, but it was the tactical thing to do. I'm sure Shane would understand, even though he was expecting her. They're great pals and work together every day. But Jessie felt she had to duck out at the last minute when Dave got the hump. She was gutted she couldn't go, but thought it was best to keep the peace.' An *EastEnders* spokesperson was keen to play down the situation. 'Jessie had a big interview to do the next night, and she just wanted to stay in and get some rest,' he said.

And this was proof, if it were needed, that the duo had, by now, become prime tabloid fodder. Sometimes, individuals come along who are so larger than life that they become characters in the nation's drama, and that was what seemed to be happening to Jessie and Dave. However trivial, nothing was left unexplored, or undiscussed. Their real-life characters were becoming just as fascinating as those in any soap.

Rather worse was to come, though, in the shape of

her court case and this was going to prove a severely testing time for both of them. In November 2003, the case was finally heard at Southend Magistrates' Court, and the best that can be said about it was that at least it was now over. Jessie admitted that she had been over the limit, but asked that she shouldn't be banned because there were special reasons for letting her off.

She was accused of driving one-and-a-half times over the limit in her £32,000 Mercedes. Jessie told the court that, on the night in question, she had just returned from Antigua and had gone to the home of her uncle and aunt, Denis and Elaine Bell, to collect Bailey, her dog, as they had been looking after him while she was away.

Once there, Jessie had a bacon and egg supper and initially decided to stay with her relatives overnight. Her Uncle Denis took her then boyfriend Andy Burton to the pub and, after they returned at 11.30pm that night, she decided to return home after all. She was stopped for speeding and given a breath test, at which point it became clear that she was over the limit. 'I was shocked,' said Jessie. 'I didn't understand. I was upset... very upset. I was hysterical, I was really crying. I didn't understand – I couldn't believe I was over the limit when I thought I'd consumed two glasses of wine.'

At first, said Jessie, she had wanted to challenge the accuracy of the toxometer used to do the breath test at

Chelmsford Police Station because she could not believe she was over the limit. But then, when she had a second appearance in court a month later, she told the Court that her Uncle Denis had put a double vodka into each glass of wine in order to cheer her up, something that he had not told her until a month after she was tried. 'He told me he had put vodka in my glasses of wine,' she said. 'I was really angry, very shocked.'

'You are telling a story about this,' said the prosecutor Charles Llewellyn, saying that Jessie was just trying to avoid disqualification. 'You have come to the Court and lied.'

'I am not a liar,' said Jessie. 'I do not lie. If I have done something wrong, I would take the punishment.'

Her Uncle Denis was also in court. 'Karen was a bit subdued that night,' he said. 'I don't know why – I thought I would cheer her up a bit. She is very comical when she has had a few drinks.' He had not owned up to what he had done earlier, he continued, because he had felt guilty about what had occurred. Jessie and he often played practical jokes on each other, he said, and he 'owed her one back'. 'It was a silly thing to do,' he continued. 'I couldn't see anything wrong with it. I feel a bit of a heel.'

'This is an attempt by you at the eleventh hour to get your niece out of trouble,' said Mr Llewellyn.

'No, sir,' Mr Bell replied.

In the event, Jessie was banned from driving for three years, fined £1,000 and ordered to pay £364 costs, although she was told she could reduce her ban by nine months if she went on a drink-drive rehabilitation course. The judge was withering in his summing up. 'On the balance of probability, Miss Wallace has fallen far short of showing these drinks were laced on that night,' said District Judge Kevin Gray. 'I do not accept that evidence and I do not find she was unaware of the amount of alcohol in her drinks.' It was a sobering end to an unedifying spectacle and Jessie's lawyer said she would appeal.

It was actually her second-drink driving conviction and it had clearly brought her down to earth with a bang. Apart from anything else, some people were beginning to speculate as to whether Jessie had a real drink problem, something she strongly denied. 'I enjoy a drink, but I'm not an alcoholic,' she said. 'I don't have a drink problem, but I regret my drink-driving conviction. I'm ashamed it happened. I now feel I'm an easy target because of it. I'm not this wild party animal. People think I'm a partygoer, who screams her head off. But I rarely go out.'

And yet Jessie still didn't seem able to calm down. Numerous stories emerged about chaos on the set; at the National Television Awards, she also launched into her fellow *EastEnders* colleague Steve McFadden, and there were further reports that she turned up worse for wear at 9.00am to film a Christmas Eve Special and had to be sent home. It might have been stress, it might have been misfortune, but Jessie's appearances in the headlines had, if anything, increased. There were dark mutterings from the BBC; Jessie was said to have been told off yet again. And while the most senior BBC bosses were keen to support their rising star, not everyone felt so sanguine.

'Just how many final chances is this woman going to have?' asked one BBC source. 'She seems to be not just drinking in the last chance saloon but living in it at the moment. It's just one thing after another. No one at *EastEnders* seems to know what to do. Jessie's important to the show – but no one is bigger than *EastEnders*.'

But still the newspaper stories went on. Jessie and Dave visited the unfortunately named Club Fuk, a gay club in Brighton, and whether or not the details were true, the visit made it into the national press yet again. The first episode, in rather a packed night, took place when she bumped into Aaron St Clair, a photographer, who asked if he could take a snap. The facts about what happened next are in dispute. St Clair alleges:

'I asked if I could take her picture, but she threw a huge tantrum,' he said. 'I really thought she was going to hit me. She went ballistic. I've never had such a bad reaction from anyone before. She was telling me where to go and being really horrible. Then all of a sudden, she turned round and said, "Come on, darling... let's have a good night and let me buy you a drink."'

Even more confusion concerns what happened next. One account was that Jessie apparently burst into the men's loos, peered over the shoulders of the men at the urinals and proceeded to give them marks out of ten. The queue for the ladies', it seemed, was too long. She then locked herself in a cubicle while Dave and a friend stood guard to make sure no one came in.

The men themselves took it in good stead. 'I was shocked she was even in the club, let alone in the men's toilets,' said one. 'But there was a massive queue for the ladies', so I suppose she couldn't be bothered to wait. All of a sudden, she burst in and put her head over my shoulder. It was a bit of a surprise, but she was very complimentary to all of us. She was so much like her character in *EastEnders* – she kept saying, "Awright, darlin'," in her East End accent.'

However, Jessie was said to be in tears, worrying what the BBC would say about the reports. Dave stood up for his lover. 'She's dead worried and feels she's been stitched up,' he said. 'Obviously, *EastEnders* wants to know what went on and Jessie is having to explain herself. She doesn't expect them to be very happy, but it would be a tragedy if she were to lose her job over this. Jessie feels like a magnet, who seems to attract trouble wherever she goes. I'm really worried about her. All this sort of stuff is making her ill. It's got to the stage where she cannot go out.'

He point-blank denied, however, the story about the men's loo. 'She went into the cubicle, locked the door, did her business and came out,' he said. 'It seems now that she cannot even go to the toilet without someone trying to stitch her up. She's a sitting duck for this kind of nonsense. We'd been for a meal and had a few drinks, but Jessie definitely wasn't drunk. She's changed since we've been together. She loves her job and is always totally professional about her work.'

Yet again, the BBC was not pleased. They were clearly desperate for all the bad publicity to go away, but, at the same time, were keen to cultivate Jessie as one of their biggest stars. 'Jessie is very popular, but these reports are causing concern,' said a BBC insider. 'Everyone knows she likes a drink.'

Jessie knew she had to take stock of the situation, and fast. She had already been suspended from *EastEnders* once, and was clearly desperate not to repeat the experience. Again and again, she was made aware of the fact that she was now public property; again and again, she saw how damaging it was for her to appear so frequently in the papers. She knew she couldn't go on as she had and she needed to improve her public image.

But this was the perfect opportunity to do so. For,

behind closed doors and away from the headlines, Jessie's romance with Dave had been developing faster than ever. The two had become inseparable, with Dave standing up for Jessie whenever she had problems, and it really did seem as if the two had at last found a soul mate in each other.

10

Holiday Time

After all the dramas and crises of the last year, it was just what Jessie and Dave needed – a break away from it all. The couple flew to a luxury resort in the Maldives for a pre-Christmas break and for the chance to celebrate their engagement properly, and appeared not to have a care in the world. In fact, they looked like any young couple in love; they enjoyed the facilities of the hotel, the beautiful scenery and the chance to relax. And it was a good time to get away, too. In England, the December weather was cold and grey; out in the Maldives, they were able to loll around in the brilliant sunshine, which in itself was enough to lift the spirits. For a very short time, they were carefree and untroubled by prying lenses.

Indeed, for the first time in months, they were able

to put everything behind them and spend some much-needed time relaxing and, on Jessie's part at least, recovering. When looking in from the outside at someone who has an extremely eventful life, it is sometimes easy to forget that it can be absolutely exhausting. Jessie wouldn't have been human if she hadn't been tired out by everything that had happened over the last year – she needed this holiday. She had been under immense strain on a number of fronts and, while she had coped very well, it had taken its toll.

The two of them settled down quickly. Indeed, they were clearly enjoying themselves. 'She must have been exhausted, as they spent the first two or three days in their hotel room,' said one onlooker. 'They're like a pair of young lovers… they really can't keep their hands off each other. They spend most of the day by the beach cuddling and giggling. Jessie looks really happy. She looked quite tired when she first arrived, but soon began to relax and enjoy herself.' It was clearly a wonderful place to relax – the hotel featured a spa with a glass floor, in order to watch the fish as you were being massaged, and a delicious seafood menu. Jessie, apparently, favoured the lobster.

The couple returned to the UK just in time for Christmas looking considerably refreshed. And once back in Britain, this calmer mood prevailed. The only controversy – for now – was pretty mild. It came when the two were spotted buying some saucy outfits in a local shop, Michelle's Fashions, in Buckhurst Hill, Essex. 'I spotted her trying on the revealing barmaid's get-up in the changing room,' said one local, who had happened to be present. 'I recognised her from the telly straight away and thought, "I bet we won't see her wearing that on screen!"

'Then I clocked her in the shop again a couple of weeks before Christmas. Her boyfriend obviously approved of the first spending spree because he was in there with her this time. They spent about half an hour browsing, pointing at the more risqué items, like a basque covered in spikes, and giggling.' The relationship was clearly still going strong although, as ever, Jessie was finding that everything she did was prone to public scrutiny.

She was now beginning to assess the events of the last year. Even by her standards, it had been pretty tempestuous stuff, given the suspension from *EastEnders*, the court case and now the engagement, but she was learning from it and attempting to make sure everything was back on track. She was also able to laugh at herself, one of the most valuable qualities when dealing with difficult times. Self-deprecation is not one of the characteristics she is most commonly associated with, but a streak of it is definitely there.

'It's definitely been fun-packed!' said Jessie of the

previous twelve months. 'The suspension was obviously a low point of the past year, but that's gone now. It was a big lesson and I've come out a lot wiser. The court case was a shock, too. But it's great to be back at work, having fantastic storylines with Michael Higgs [Andy] and Shane Richie [Alfie] and meeting Dave, of course.' Every cloud, it seemed, had a silver lining.

And now that all the drama was out of the way, the two were finally able to plan ahead. Not that they were rushing into anything. 'We haven't discussed the wedding yet,' said Jessie. 'It's just lovely being with someone who I think the world of and who thinks the world of me. He looks after me and we're just totally happy together.' It was very much a time for bonding; now that they could finally relax, they were able to enjoy their relationship all the more.

And it was, after all, the first time since they'd got together that they were able to do so. Given that they'd met at the beginning of the court case and had weathered a fair bit together since then, their relationship had only rarely been able to develop in peace. Now they were finally getting the chance to make up for all the upheaval of the past year.

And as they basked in the glow of their engagement, the two were now ready to share with the world how it had come about. The proposal itself had taken place when they were having a break in New York. Asked if it had come as a shock, Jessie replied, 'No, because we both know how we feel about each other, it was very mutual. But we're still on our honeymoon period, that's why we haven't discussed the wedding yet. It's just nice that we both know how we feel about each other.' Nonetheless, she was clearly looking forward to married life.

And while the engagement might not have been a shock, Dave had still arranged everything carefully beforehand. The agreement to get married might have been a mutual one, but he was still determined to make sure the proposal was memorable. He also managed to include something that would appeal to Jessie's innermost desires, something that related to her ideal man.

'Dave's really great with surprises,' said Jessie. 'He organised this huge one for me when we went to New York. A car picked us up from our hotel at three in the morning and took us to the airport for a flight to Memphis [the home of Elvis Presley]. I'm a really massive Elvis fan and we were in Elvis-land for two days. I didn't have a clue that he'd planned it! He's just so considerate like that, it's lovely.' It was a sign of the strength of their relationship back then – the two really were keen to do as much for each other as they could.

As it happened, though, the proposal actually had to wait until they were back in the Big Apple. 'I took her to Graceland as a surprise and I was going to do it there...' said Dave, '... but I was too wrapped up in the Elvis experience so he did it when we were in New York,' continued Jessie. 'I knew he was going to do it and, in the end, he asked me in the hotel we were staying in: 60 Thompson in Soho. We were there during the blackout.' It made the occasion all the more memorable still.

It seemed to be a sign that Jessie was at last ready to settle down. After all, this was the ideal time to do so – she was in her early thirties, was becoming established in her career and had had enough difficult romantic experiences to know the value of finding the right person, as Dave very much seemed to be at the time. Although she enjoyed having fun out and about, she also enjoyed home life, domesticity and comfort. She had a growing menagerie of pets – which could in itself be interpreted as displaying some kind of maternal streak – a nice house, a good life. It was the right time to lead a calmer existence and getting married seemed to be part of the plan.

And then, of course, there was all the fun of the engagement ring to sort out. 'I designed it and a friend of mine made it for me, which took a couple of weeks,' said Jessie in an interview at the time. 'I really wanted something that was Art Deco. I had an aquamarine stone first of all, but it wasn't appropriate and it looked a bit gaudy, so I had this made… ' Costing about £14,000, it was a very tasteful ring – much like the rest of Jessie's wardrobe, in fact. She might have been as strong-willed as her on-screen character, but their tastes were definitely very different.

And, of course, art was imitating life. The engagement had actually come at about the same time as Kat was getting married to Andy in *EastEnders*, which meant that Jessie had a pretend wedding at about the same time as she was thinking of a real one. The contrast felt a little odd. 'I think it's every girl's dream to walk down the aisle, so filming it felt really bizarre,' said Jessie. 'Standing there in this beautiful corseted dress, arm-in-arm with Derek, who plays my dad – and he really is like a dad – and then they start playing a wedding march and I'm walking down the aisle. It was a weird feeling. The director wanted me to look excited and I genuinely was. It was a fantastic feeling. They spent so much money on this wedding that everything felt so real.'

The on-screen wedding, incidentally, was yet another sign of Jessie's standing within *EastEnders* itself. The storyline was one of the crowd-pullers, one of the big numbers, as it were, designed to bring in publicity and viewers, and it delivered on both fronts. And, not for the first time – nor the last – Jessie, or Kat, was in the middle of it all.

It was a concrete sign of her success on the show; she

could shoulder the really major stories, while bringing in the viewers. And, of course, it was a virtuous circle. The more Jessie was given these central scenes, the greater her popularity became; the greater her popularity became, the more she was given these pivotal moments. And it was a sign that she would be capable of so much more.

Of course, there was her own wedding to think about and plan for as well. Jessie had certainly dreamt about her wedding day when she was a child, and a typically romantic gloss she had put on it, too. 'There's this church around the corner from me in Old Street in London and it's got no roof on it – it was bombed during the Blitz,' she said. 'I used to walk past it as a little girl. It's got these trees growing in it and I had this vision of having a medieval wedding at midnight with fairy lights, but they've put a roof on the church now, so that's gone out of the window!'

The two were clearly very happy about spending their lives together. Asked what she was looking forward to most, Jessie replied, 'I think the companionship and being together all the time, doing things together – you're never bored because you're always doing stuff together, it's lovely. I do think I've found my soul mate, definitely.' It certainly appeared so – Jessie and Dave were constantly in each other's company and seemed without a care in the world.

'The security, the companionship, the fact you have something to come home to,' Dave chipped in, when he was asked the same question. 'It's definitely nice to have someone always there for you.' And at that stage, they really were there for one another. Dave was extremely protective of his new fiancée, while Jessie rather enjoyed being protected. And they still gained enormous enjoyment from each other's company, to say nothing of the fact that they found one another extremely attractive. There was no sign at all of any of the ructions that were to come.

On the subject of children, however, they were initially a bit coy. 'We haven't thought that far ahead,' said Jessie. 'I've got three dogs and I think that's enough at the moment! [The menagerie had been added to over the years.] And I've got four nephews and one niece.' She was a very devoted aunt, though, perhaps a sign that she really was ready for one of her own. 'We haven't discussed kids yet,' added Dave. 'It's gone through my mind a couple of times, but we haven't really talked about it.'

They may not have talked about it, but it didn't take long before they were doing something about it – on Valentine's Day 2004, to be precise. Having decided to get engaged, the two were clearly thinking along the lines of starting a family, even if they hadn't been quite ready to talk about it publicly – and so they did just that. Although it seemed very early in their relationship to be considering a family, they had, by now, been together for a while. They had got engaged in the autumn of 2003 and Jessie didn't conceive until early 2004; their relationship seemed solid and stable, with children clearly the next step to take. So why not?

As ever, in their own inimitable style, the two went about telling everyone that they were expecting a child. Revealing she was pregnant, Jessie could not help but be slightly giggly as she explained how it had all come about. It had been a romantic evening that had become more romantic still, with the happy result that they now were able to share with the world.

'We're both thrilled, but the fact that it happened on Valentine's Day makes it perfect,' she said. 'That evening Dave bought me flowers, then took me to the West End for a champagne dinner at the Marco Pierre White restaurant, Criterion. But, really, we couldn't wait to get home and so we left for a celebration on our own – in the shower! Now we are expecting a baby and we couldn't be happier. In fact, the only time in my life I've felt this good was when I landed my part in *EastEnders*.'

And it was to be as big an upheaval as landing the part of Kat had been. Jessie's life had changed beyond all description when she went from complete unknown to one of the most famous faces in the country and the only kind of change on that scale that was remotely conceivable was pregnancy. It was to change everything for ever; her maternal feelings were to have full expression, as she herself realised. She would be looking after a baby in a few short months from now. Just as she sometimes could scarcely believe she'd landed a past in *EastEnders*, so now it sometimes seemed incredible that she was pregnant. But she was – and there was no going back.

But Jessie being Jessie, there was no time for introspection. This news was to be greeted as cheerily as everything else, in the robust manner for which she was becoming known. She was also in characteristically jokey mood about naming the baby, and cited Brooklyn Beckham – named after where he was conceived – as one possible source of inspiration. 'We both like unusual names and, although the baby's surname will be Morgan, Dave won't get much of a look in about the first name because that's up to me,' she said. 'If it's a girl, she'll be Iris; and if it's a boy, Elvis, after my hero. But as we were at home in East London when I conceived, I'm considering Wanstead.'

This entire episode, of course, heralded a complete turn around in circumstances. It seemed merely minutes earlier that Jessie had been a wild child; now she was expecting a child herself and ecstatically happy about it. This was proof, if any were needed, that she really was set on turning her life around; domesticity seemed only a step away. And yet, given Jessie's tendency to imbue her life with drama, the advent of her pregnancy seemed yet another extraordinary event in what was, by any standards, a pretty extraordinary life.

She continued to bubble over with anticipation, utterly thrilled about the turn of events. 'I'm really excited,' she said. 'We are very happy about our news. It is something I've always wanted. It's amazing to think that, by November, I will have my own little person to look after.' There was no indication at all back then that all might not go quite as smoothly as planned: all Jessie seemed to be concerned about was that her life had come back on track completely in the last year.

And she was well aware of the fact that she'd been fortunate. Twelve months previously, she had been facing problems at work, a barrage of bad publicity and the lack of a happy relationship. Now she was enjoying the flip side of that coin. 'This time last year, things were not good for me,' she said in 2004. 'I was really on a downward spiral. I wish I could have looked ahead and seen how my life would turn out because then I would never have got so depressed. But the truth is, when I met Dave it was a terrible time – I was in court for drink-driving, which was such a stupid and irresponsible thing to do. But at least something good came out of it… him.'

The way she spoke about Dave was extremely

touching. Jessie might have been the big star, but she was also as capable of falling in love as the next woman, and she had clearly done so now. 'I never imagined Dave would fancy me, let alone end up being the father of my baby!' she said. 'But he took me under his wing and I've stayed there ever since. Dave was my knight in shining armour then, and he is definitely the one now. I'm so happy I have to keep reminding myself because it seems too good to be true. I'm 32 this year and I thought I'd end up an old spinster smelling of cats!'

If truth be told, there was never much danger of that. Jessie was a bona fide sex symbol, who attracted men effortlessly, as she had so often done in the past. But her romantic history had been a turbulent one. There was the unnamed actor who had been so violent towards her; Paul, whom she was truly in love with, but who did not like the publicity surrounding dating a television star; and various others who, if truth be told, had seemed to see Jessie as a way of promoting themselves. But it was different with Dave. He had stuck by Jessie during one of the most difficult periods of her life and they had come through it together. It was no wonder both of them felt so happy.

Dave was equally ecstatic and keen to emphasise the fact that the couple's party lifestyle was now a thing of the past. He enjoyed going out and taking part in the good life just as much as his fiancée, but he was equally aware of the importance of settling down now that there was a baby on the way. 'We celebrated our good news, but Jessie stuck to mineral water,' he said. 'She's not drinking any more. It's hard to convey how happy we're both feeling. It is great news about the baby; it's really brilliant. We're both thrilled and delighted.'

Indeed, it had not been unexpected, either. Once they had got engaged, it turned out, the two had been keen to try for a baby, and were utterly delighted when their endeavours proved to be a success. 'It was planned and we're keeping our fingers crossed that everything will go well,' said Dave. 'Jessie's very, very happy and looking forward to becoming a mum. She's had a tough few months but all that's behind her now. It's been really difficult keeping quiet for the past few weeks, but it's wonderful now we've been given the all-clear by doctors.'

But, as ever, the problems involved with being a celebrity dogged Jessie even here, too. It was very difficult to keep her private life under wraps. As soon as she suspected she might be pregnant, she'd wanted to find out for sure – but she couldn't get the necessary testing kit in person in case she was seen. 'I had suspicions that I might be expecting, just like any woman would,' she said. 'But I was too embarrassed to go to the chemist to buy a pregnancy test in case anyone recognised me. So Dave went.'

And there was another element, too; if anyone had recognised her, they might well have sold the story to the newspapers, whether she was pregnant or not, or at the very least gone public with the news before the couple was ready. Any number of problems might have arisen then, not least because not only would Jessie have wanted to inform her family and friends first, but she would have wanted to consult her bosses at work, too. As it turned out, the problems were averted, and she and Dave managed to start planning their future quietly... but it was not without hiccups. Despite the upside, it really is not always easy being a star.

But, problems about people spotting her aside, Jessie was pregnant and the two of them could hardly believe it. 'As soon as we saw it was positive, we were jumping around the living room whooping!' said Jessie. 'Then the news sank in and we cried with joy. I believe in fate and that things happen for a reason and I know Dave is the one for me, so the timing couldn't be better. We've been together a year and I'm at a place in my life where everything feels right.'

The duo were over the moon. It really did seem as if everything was finally coming together at last – marriage, which they decided to postpone until after the baby was born, and motherhood. The past was truly in the past. And Jessie had had plenty of practice as far as motherhood was concerned; she was, after all, an aunt five times over, and was close to her nephews and niece, as well as being strongly supportive towards her sister. She had helped Joanne with the pressures of motherhood and looked after the little ones herself, too. She was fully prepared for when her own child came along.

And they had waited a while to be certain that everything was going to be all right, not easy for two such ebullient characters as Jessie and Dave, but, in the end, they were finally able to disclose their news. In due course, the two told their families, followed by friends and cast members, with Shane Richie the first to know. He was Jessie's great chum on the set and he rose to the occasion magnificently.

'Shane has been singing Elvis songs to my belly,' said Jessie. 'He was the first person on *EastEnders* that I told, so he's known for a while and he's been great. He's really been looking after me and he was so pleased for Dave as well. Leslie Grantham, who plays Dirty Den, has also been giving me plenty of advice – most importantly, he told me not to cross my legs because it would give me varicose veins.' It was indeed excellent advice, but it was not all Leslie confined himself to saying in the course of that month, as Jessie was later to find out.

And if she hadn't told the world, the world might well have guessed. Jessie's chest, always one of her good features, had increased dramatically, and people were beginning to think something was going on. And then, on top of that, she was starting to develop cravings. 'A couple of girls in the costume department had already noticed that I was putting on weight,' said Jessie. 'Then, when I told them I was expecting, they admitted they'd guessed. Now they're loving it and they're busy buying loads of maternity clothes for Kat. Dave's also pretty thrilled that my boobs have grown so much!'

This was slightly tricky timing as far as filming was concerned, however, but in the end it worked out. Jessie/Kat was yet again in the middle of one of the show's jaw-dropping storylines: in this case, Andy, the man Kat had jilted at the altar, had offered her £10,000 to sleep with him. All in the interests of getting good old Alfie out of debt, she agreed to it. So it was an interesting time for her to announce her pregnancy, but the *EastEnders*' bosses were very good and utterly supportive of their star. After all, Jessie was seen not only as one of the major stars of the show, but as one of the BBC's great white hopes. So it was not surprising that they tried to accommodate her when she explained she was having a child.

'I did have a little moment's panic over what would happen with work,' said Jessie. 'I was worried about what they would say and that my timing might be off, but they've been great – they really have. We haven't decided yet if a pregnancy storyline will be written into *EastEnders*, but it won't matter if it's not. Kat is always standing behind the bar at the Queen Vic at the moment, so the bump will be easy to hide.' That was as maybe – Jessie's whole shape was changing – but clearly everyone was happy with what had been agreed.

The couple's happiness was really very touching. They were seen sitting on a park bench studying the twelve-week scan outside Portland Hospital, where Jessie was to have the baby, a London celebrity favourite that has played host to, among others, Victoria Beckham, Zoë Ball, Elizabeth Hurley and Sophie Wessex. 'Both of them looked really, really happy, as if they didn't have a care in the world,' said one onlooker.

Jessie and Dave themselves were delighted with the results of the scan, which showed that everything was in order. 'It's every mother's worry that there could be something wrong with their baby, but so far everything is all right,' she said. 'We don't know if it's a boy or a girl, but we know it's not twins. We also got to see its little arms and legs, and it looked like it was waving to us, which was amazing. There were more tears then. I haven't felt the baby kick yet, that doesn't come for a couple more months, but I am getting bigger out front… there again, I've always had a bit of a belly.'

More than ever, Jessie was showing herself to be a role model for women. There was no consideration then about not putting on too much weight during her pregnancy and, indeed, when the baby did finally make an appearance, Jessie was not one of those women who lost all the weight and more just weeks after giving birth. She was a totally natural woman, with a natural pregnancy, and she wasn't trying to be a superwoman – she was just trying to be sensible and do what was right.

And pregnancy suited her. It may be a cliché to say it, but Jessie genuinely developed that bloom that some expectant mothers have. And whatever feelings of tiredness she might have had, she didn't let it affect her work; the show was as important to her as it ever had been and so she soldiered on, gripping as many fans as she had done before. Indeed, it was quite remarkable how well she coped; as ever, she was showing that under the greatest stresses and strains, she was more than capable of delivering great work when she needed to.

Like any new mother, though, she did confess to some worries. 'I am slightly scared – after all, this is for the rest of my life, but hopefully I'll be a good mum,' she said. 'But I know Dave will be a fantastic dad because he's so caring and he gets gushy over other people's babies. He's also been buying baby books and keeps reading bits out to me and telling me what I can and cannot eat. We'll know by November, I'm sure.'

It was a huge break with the past. And, as Jessie herself said, there was no going back. The baby was on its way, she was going to be a mother and a whole new phase of her life was about to begin. She might have been scared, but she was also wildly excited and looking forward to whatever the future held in store. And the future certainly seemed bright. She had continued to make waves as an actress, had continued to impress her bosses, had continued to enthral her growing army of fans and had at last her personal life sorted out. And this was just the right age for motherhood – she was thirty-two, which meant that she'd had plenty of time to enjoy her youth, but she was still young enough not to be too exhausted by the physical and mental demands of carrying a child.

But when did the course of Jessie's life ever run smoothly? Yet another furore was just round the corner but for once, it had nothing to do with our heroine, who was now on her best behaviour and appearing as a model actress and conscientious mother-to-be on the set. She was living carefully, as befitted her condition, taking care of herself and getting ready for the arrival of her child. Rather, it was the actions of one of her co-stars that caused a huge fuss – the débâcle lasted for weeks and is remembered to this day. And who was at the centre of this particular storm? Leslie Grantham.

11
Playing Dirty

As scandals go, the actual events were relatively innocuous, but the row they provoked caused a sensation. And it was certainly exceedingly embarrassing for the man involved.

Just one year earlier, after a fourteen-year absence, Leslie Grantham had finally been lured back on to the programme that had made him a household name. He was to reprise the role of Den Watts, better known as Dirty Den – cad, heartbreaker, father of his daughter's friend's child and server of divorce papers upon the lovely Angie, in one of the most watched episodes of any British television soap. Dirty Den was back.

Unfortunately, one year on, Leslie, now fifty-seven, seemed to be taking his nickname a little too seriously. Several Sunday newspapers found out that, in the privacy of his dressing room at the *EastEnders* studios in

Elstree, he was indulging in a slightly unusual hobby – he appeared to be exposing himself to an online friend, while at the same time completely rubbishing fellow members of the cast. The BBC was emphatically not amused.

One of these activities alone would have been enough to cause outrage, but the two together ensured that the story dominated the headlines for days. On top of that was the issue of whether he was using licence-payers' money to log on and misbehave. If he had sat down and planned how to create a sensationalist scandal, he couldn't have done better than this.

And, it must be said, Leslie had been a little unwise. He had been chatting to a twenty-three-year-old blonde, known only as 'Amanda', and he had not held back about his feelings for the rest of the cast. The long-serving (and long-suffering) Wendy Richard was called a 'wanker', Jessie was a 'vile dog', Shane Richie was 'big-headed and self-infatuated', and Kim Medcalf 'a block of wood... thick'. He then went on to suggest that some cast members took drugs.

It is safe to say that his fellow cast members were not pleased to hear what had apparently been going on behind their backs. Indeed, they were absolutely livid, with some calling on the BBC to give him the sack. 'If Grantham gets away with this, there will be a revolt,' said one insider on the show. 'The cast told producers it cannot be one rule for him and another for them. He has to be disciplined or this could lead to the cast walking out. Even some of the actors not due in today made the point of coming in to complain. They told producers they do not want to work with him any more.'

This showed the depth of the feeling involved. It is very unusual for actors to be so openly censorious of one another but, of course, not only were they personally wounded by what Leslie had said, but his actions also reflected very badly on the show. No one might have been bigger than the Square but, as various others had discovered over the years, personal misbehaviour casts a blight over everyone else as well. And the particular nature of this episode which, to put it kindly, was squalid, made everyone else more resentful still.

Leslie himself was well aware of how foolish he'd been. He tried to quell his colleagues' anger by calling a meeting with them and told Shane and Jessie personally that 'you are a pleasure to work with'. He then added that the woman on the other end of the webcam made up the comments, before going on to say, 'Let's all be professional about this... we've all got to work together.'

But it didn't wash. Everyone else was so angry that a further, more public apology was needed and, aware what a tricky position he was in, Leslie obliged. In a statement issued through the BBC, he said:

'I would like to unreservedly apologise to the cast and crew of *EastEnders* and the BBC for the embarrassment that has been caused by recent newspaper allegations. I would like to also say sorry and pay personal tribute to Kim Medcalf, Wendy Richard, Shane Richie and Jessie Wallace in particular, who have been caught up in the results of my deplorable actions.

'I very much regret that a moment's stupidity has cast a shadow over what I consider one of Britain's best shows, of which I'm thoroughly proud to be a part. I am wholeheartedly ashamed of my behaviour and feel that I have let down my colleagues, as well as my friends and family. In some small recompense, I intend to make a donation to charity as a mark of my apology. Now I'd like some time to show my family the love and support they have shown me over the last few days.'

His family were, indeed, standing right behind him; Leslie's wife Jane put on a very public show of support, kissing her husband on the doorstep of their home as he left for work on Sunday.

The BBC, meanwhile, issued a statement of its own:

'Anything that exposes the programme to embarrassment and any abuse of BBC resources is taken very seriously by the BBC,' it said. 'However, we do appreciate Leslie's sincere expression of regret and his decision to make a contribution to charity. We do not intend to make any further public statements about this matter.'

Jessie, however, was not exactly in a mood to forgive and forget. Onlookers revealed that Leslie had tried to apologise to her in person and made the mistake of trying to touch her stomach. She was having none of it and retorted, 'Push off! Don't you dare touch me.'

Someone who had witnessed the encounter made it clear she had a lot of support. 'Jessie felt very vulnerable,' he said. 'Leslie is a big chap. He was very close to her and he kept thrusting a piece of paper forward. Jessie kept her dignity – she spoke for the lot of us.' It must have been enormously cheering for her when, shortly afterwards, she won Sexiest Female Award at the British Soap Awards. She attended the ceremony with Dave, looking glamorous in a black trouser suit with a fur collar. Her appearance, more than anything else, was answer enough to Leslie's unkind remarks.

But it had clearly hit her rather hard. 'I don't do a lot of scenes with Leslie,' said Jessie, when asked how she was coping with working with him. 'But it's fine. We just get on with our jobs. Who knows if he said it? But if he did,

I'd like to forget about it. It's not very nice to see a picture of yourself with the words "vile dog" printed underneath.' She didn't say a great deal more, but then, she didn't have to. The public was firmly behind her.

The problem for the BBC was this – on the one hand, it took firm action against anyone who could be said to bring it into disrepute, while on the other, Leslie was actually very popular with the viewers. His return to the show had generated a huge amount of publicity, and brought back many viewers who had left the show years before.

His character was also a good add to the mix, to say nothing of the fact that it linked the modern-day *EastEnders* to its hugely successful début twenty years earlier. Clearly, the BBC didn't want to get rid of their valuable asset but, at the same time, his offences were deemed to be so severe that something more had to be done.

And so, in May 2004, it was announced that, like so many before him, Leslie was to be suspended from *EastEnders* without pay for two months. 'Leslie knew he was going to be punished,' said one BBC source. 'But he is just lucky that he was allowed to keep his job. He was told in no uncertain terms that he had shamed the show and made a fool of himself. He had made the cast members a laughing stock and embarrassed them.'

The BBC was forced to make a further announcement: 'A disciplinary meeting did take place, but we won't be commenting on it further because it is an internal matter,' it said. It was caught between a rock and a hard place. There was no way they were going to win this one, whatever they did.

Of course, Leslie was not the first person who had had to suffer the indignity of suspension. Jessie had had to deal with it, too, and it had actually come in the nick of time for her, as she herself confessed. Her behaviour had been on the verge of getting out of hand, but it stopped her in her tracks before it was too late. 'It really was a kick in the teeth,' she said. 'I will admit, before I was suspended I was a little sod. I would turn up late, I was so blasé about stuff... I took it for granted. Nothing was in perspective. I don't think I was very popular at the time on set. The two months' suspension gave me two months to think about what I was doing.'

Indeed, Jessie had fully appreciated that she had had a second chance. In many ways, she had changed; she was aware of the constant interest in her and that anything she said or did in public was likely to end up in the papers. She was also conscious of the fact that, while this level of interest could be difficult to deal with, it was the price she had to pay for the position she held in the public eye. As she herself said, she'd be more worried if people ignored her than anything else, but it did mean she had to keep her wilder side in check.

Not that she had completely calmed her rather hot temper. The early calm induced by her pregnancy began to give way to her more usual fiery self and, in no time at all, she found herself embroiled in a row with, of all things, a garden centre. Indeed, feelings ran so high, she was banned from its premises.

The problem, it appeared, was that she had bought forty-six conifer trees for £1,610, three of which died, at which point she rang the centre and made her feelings known in no uncertain terms. She tore a strip off the various people involved, working herself up into an absolute fury.

'Wallace was trying to use her position and went absolutely ballistic,' said Andrew Brown, the owner of Brown's Garden Centre. 'She spoke to one of my employees, demanding ten free trees, and began shouting and ranting at her for no reason. The poor girl was shell-shocked. I phoned Wallace to say I was happy to replace the trees, but she again said she wanted ten free ones.

'Bawling at the top of her voice, she kept saying effing this and effing that. It was a tirade of pure filth and seemed to go on for ages. Later, a PR person rang to tell me that the phone conversation had been taped and that she was going to take me to court. But I don't care who she is, I treat everyone the same. I don't know whether Kat Moon is Jessie Wallace or the other way round.'

Everyone involved seemed a little shaken. 'The

conifers are her pride and joy,' said one of her neighbours. 'They were planted behind the garden railings to give some privacy. The dead conifers really stick out because they have gone yellow and wilted. It has obviously wound Jessie up.' That was putting it mildly. Jessie herself was cool about it afterwards. 'She is taking legal action against the garden centre for supplying faulty goods,' said a spokesperson. 'She denies being rude to staff.'

Shortly afterwards, there was another row, this time with her co-star Elaine Lordan, who was due to leave the show in the summer. On this occasion, it was Elaine who had an even hotter temper than Jessie, and who started the row. Apparently, after Jessie kept forgetting her lines, Elaine began shouting at her. Jessie apologised and said that her pregnancy was making her forgetful, but Elaine wasn't exactly sympathetic.

'Why don't you stop bleeding apologising and learn your lines instead?' she demanded, continuing, 'You think you're the queen on the show.'

'At least I'm still on the show,' Jessie replied.

In many ways, it was a shame; the two had been good friends when they first joined the show and had gone out with each other a lot. Indeed, it was Elaine who featured with Jessie in the infamous picture of the two of them dancing around in the street together taken in the early years. But Elaine had had her own problems over the years, culminating in the fact that the producers could deal with it no longer. After an exceedingly eventful four years, she was off for pastures new. And that is one possible cause of the rift between them – Elaine was leaving, while Jessie had pulled herself back from the brink.

It didn't help that the spat had happened publicly, too. 'They had a huge bust-up in front of everyone,' said an onlooker who had witnessed the row. 'Jessie apologised when she forgot her lines the first time. When she apologised again, she jokingly said it must be down to her hormones as she's pregnant.

'Everyone laughed it off, apart from Elaine. She didn't find it amusing at all and just laid into her. Elaine was shouting and screaming at Jessie, and didn't care who heard it. You could have cut the atmosphere with a knife. Jessie remarked to the crew afterwards that Elaine was behaving as if drunk. And Elaine was moaning to the crew how she had had enough of Jessie.' It was a relationship that had clearly broken down.

Worse, however, was to come. Bust-ups with co-stars were one thing – and this was not the first time the former friends had had words – but, rather more worryingly, cracks began to show in Jessie's relationship with Dave. This was a time when the two should have been coming closer together and planning for the birth of their child, to say nothing of their wedding afterwards, and yet, increasingly, it began to appear that something had soured between them.

Jessie was seen without her engagement ring, although friends said that this was because her ring finger was swollen; and then, more seriously, there were reports that Dave had moved out. Of course, pregnancy is a notoriously difficult time for a couple but, even so, real problems in the relationship were beginning to emerge. And, as time passed, they were only to get worse.

The trouble began with a huge row, in which Jessie told Dave she thought he wasn't committed enough to the baby. It then escalated, to the extent that Dave actually moved out. Friends close to them tried to play it down, but it was obvious that something was very wrong. And the speed with which the relationship began to break down also took everyone by surprise; just a couple of months previously, they had been looking forward to building a future together.

'Having a baby is always traumatic for a young couple and the stresses have taken their toll,' said one source close to the couple. 'Jessie's bewildered and upset. Her emotions have been up and down during her pregnancy because it's such a major event in her life. We all hope they make it up with each other – and soon. He's not moved out… he's just stayed away for a few nights.'

Initially, they appeared to patch things up; Dave was seen at the couple's home again, while the ring reappeared on Jessie's finger. Jessie herself refused to comment on the rumours, while Dave's mother Barbara said, 'It's absolutely ridiculous to say there is a problem – they are fine.'

But the reunion was short-lived. Much worse was to come, and very shortly, too, for a friend of Dave's, Winston Rollock, who had done some work on Jessie's home, then sold a story about her to a newspaper, making all kinds of allegations about her lifestyle, including stories about drinking and sex. He also said that she was rude about other cast members. Jessie was absolutely devastated, said she would sue and called the engagement off for good.

'I just feel like I've been totally trodden on. How much worse can things get?' she asked, rather understandably, given the circumstances. 'The past days have been awful, absolutely awful. I am terrified that all the pain and upset I have been feeling goes straight to my baby. This baby is the most important thing in the world and I'd hate anything to happen.'

Poor Jessie had got used to people she knew selling stories about her in the past, but this was different. The boyfriends who'd kissed and sold had only been brief blips on the radar; this, however, was much closer to home. Rollock had been, if not a friend of Jessie's, then at least a friend of Dave's, and his behaviour had a devastating effect. An emotive person at the best of times, this was also appalling timing, occurring right in the middle of Jessie's pregnancy. It was hardly surprising she felt devastated.

'The truth is, all this stress has made me ill,' she said. 'I'm five-and-a-half months pregnant and I'm very emotional. On Saturday night, I thought I was going to have a breakdown. I was crying so much I was in pain. I don't need this crap wrapped round me any more. It's just best for me and Dave to split because I need to be on my own. What I need is my friends around me and I just need to get some normality back. Basically, I can't take it any more, especially being pregnant – I'm worried about the health of my baby.'

It was a shock to everyone, but now that the split had actually happened, it quickly became obvious that the couple were not going to get back together. When relationships come under pressure, as they invariably do when there's a baby involved, it sometimes highlights weaknesses and problems that would otherwise have remained hidden. That certainly seemed to be the case here.

When Jessie was asked if it was over for good, she replied, 'I should think so. It's gone too far, too much has happened. I just don't know who to trust any more. I just need to make a fresh start. My problems with Dave have been going on for a while and we thought it was best to part. Every child needs a father and I know Dave will be supportive, I know he will. I've got the utmost respect for him... we were engaged and I want him to be there and he wants to be there. I'm not going to allow myself to be down in the dumps because I know my baby will pick up on the bad vibes. Every time I feel it kick, it brings it all back to reality. I can't wait for the baby to be born, I'm so excited. I'm really looking forward to it.'

Jessie was not, however, prepared to forgive Rollock and, sick of the stories that so frequently came out about her, decided that this time she would talk to her lawyers. 'It's not very nice when allegations are made against you that are untrue,' she said. 'I'm taking legal action. It's got to the point, after four years in *EastEnders*, when I can't keep taking this. I'm sick and tired of it. Things like this rip people to bits. I haven't really spoken to Dave over this.'

Her devastation was understandable. Rollock had been privy to her private life and, while Jessie just about managed to cope with the constant attention when she was out in public, having someone close to the inner sanctum speaking out was just too much. Neither had she – nor anyone else – seen this one coming. In some instances, Jessie had learned that people might try to provoke her or sell stories that didn't bear a very close relationship to the truth, but this really was different.

'I trusted this guy [Rollock],' Jessie said. 'I didn't allow him into my life but he had keys to my home. He was in my house for eight months doing my stairs and it got to the point where I thought, "I wish I had never got him to do this." When I went through how much I gave him, I told him, "Are you aware of how much I have given you? If you had quoted me that much at the beginning, I would have said leave it."'

Indeed, it might well have been the fall-out from the work that prompted Rollock to sell his story to the press. Jessie was not pleased with the standard of the work he'd done, and made that clear, too. She said, 'I thought, "This guy is not getting any more money from me," and I told him that. He was a friend of Dave's. I paid him £15,000. The Jack Daniels' stuff was nonsense – It's not me, I can't even walk into a smoky room. I've [also] got the utmost respect for all cast members. If I've got anything to say, I'd say it to them. I'd never say that about Barbara Windsor.'

The strain, unsurprisingly, was getting to her more and more. Jessie had been the subject of constant rumours and innuendo practically from the day she walked on to the *EastEnders* set and, despite the rows and dramas that punctuated her life, had coped with it all pretty well. But now that she was pregnant, something had changed and, shortly after the Rollock episode, she was admitted to the Portland Hospital suffering from stress. Concerned doctors then signed her off work for two weeks. Dave, it must be said, was at her side.

'Obviously, Jessie is very concerned and the health of her baby is imperative,' said a friend. 'The doctors told her she must slow down. They have admitted her partly because of a medical condition which could affect the baby, and partly due to stress. The last few months have been extremely difficult for Jessie and there is a worry this may have impacted on her pregnancy. She was extremely upset when one of Dave's friends sold a story about her and has found the whole thing extremely hard. It looks like Jessie and the baby will be fine, but this has been a real scare for her and Dave. She just needs to rest and take it easy for a while.'

In a life like Jessie's, this was never going to be easy. She was accustomed to living life at such a pace that any slowing down might have been difficult for her to accept, but now there was the baby to think about, too. And so, as best she could, she did sit back and have a short rest, after which she was able to return to *EastEnders*. The pregnancy, thankfully, went ahead with few further concerns.

In the middle of all this, some very much needed support and light relief came along. The support came from the BBC, who now decided to make it clear quite how highly they valued their star; they made it known that Jessie was to star in a prime-time drama outside her work in *EastEnders*.

'Jessie has been told that she will be taken care of by the BBC and she has a bright future,' said a source within the Corporation. 'Jessie loves *EastEnders* and has no plans to leave at the moment, but she is very keen to explore other opportunities. She was in talks to appear in other BBC projects and they will go forward when the baby is born. Obviously, she will be keen to get stuck back into *EastEnders*. She is looking forward to becoming a mum, but is anxious to prove she can enjoy work and home life.'

The light relief came from a completely different source; her younger sister Danielle, who was by now twenty-one. She had been working as a member of ground staff for bmi at Heathrow Airport, but decided to give it up in favour of a career in modelling. To that end, she posed for some Page 3 pictures, and said that Jessie had told her, 'You can be the new Jordan.' Jessie was utterly supportive to her little sister; Danielle, in turn, hero-worshipped her sister and was happy to tell that to the world.

Indeed, after the behaviour of Rollock, encountered so recently by Jessie, Danielle's news couldn't have come at a better time. 'She said, "That's just absolutely brilliant. I'm so proud of you – I know you've got what it takes to do really well,'" Danielle related. 'Jessie thinks I can be a big-name model like Jordan or Melinda Messenger. I have her full blessing.'

She added that the only person who wasn't pleased with her new career path was her boyfriend. Taking a leaf out of her sister's book, she promptly ended the relationship. 'I'm glad we split,' she said. 'He was holding me back, he stopped me from modelling. He didn't want other men admiring me.'

And, given all the nonsense that was written about Jessie, she finally received unqualified praise from her sister, which must have been more than welcome. 'Jessie has always been very protective of me,' said Danielle. 'She always stands up for me, but she's nothing like Kat – she's a lot more diplomatic. Where Kat would go storming in, Jessie thinks things through a lot more. She gives really good advice. I don't think Jessie is scary… but no one would dare start on me if she was about. She's my best friend and protector. We're like soul mates and she isn't anything like the way she's portrayed. We are really close friends – she doesn't tell me what to do.'

Indeed, the two were extremely close. Jessie was not alone in looking forward to having her baby; the rest of the family couldn't wait for the new arrival, too. 'I know Jessie is really looking forward to being a mum,' said

Danielle. 'I idolise Jessie. To have got where she is without anyone else's help is amazing. She is an inspiration to me.'

Physically, the two are actually quite dissimilar; Danielle is blonde to Jessie's brunette. But the photographer Alan Strutt, who took her first Page 3 pictures, somehow made some kind of connection. 'There was something familiar about her and I kept saying, "You really remind me of someone,"' he said. 'Eventually, she told me about Jessie. I would certainly never have guessed. They have similar eyes, but a very different look overall – and one is blonde and the other dark. Danielle was a natural in front of the camera. She has a fantastic smile and striking eyes. She'll go far.'

And, as so many people in Jessie's life, Danielle was also beginning to experience something of what life is like as a celebrity, although in her case, of course, she was actually entering the world of showbusiness, too. The talk about signing up as a model had begun before she'd actually left her previous job, with the result that a certain buzz was beginning to develop around her, one that she herself found quite strange.

'All the passengers were asking to be checked in by me,' Danielle confessed, before going on to say that she didn't want to be drawn into the more downmarket side of the business. 'I don't want to come across as tacky and I'm not interested in bitchy feuds,' she said. 'I really admire Jordan – I think she has a great image, but I don't understand why Jodie Marsh called Abi Titmuss cheap. That was hypocritical, especially as she is hardly squeaky clean herself. Jodie has a bit of work to do in the image department – I wouldn't want to be put in the same category as her.'

It was all light-hearted stuff, but an enormous relief for Jessie, not least as she needed something to take her mind off the recent rows and break-up from Dave. Occasionally, it can be a relief to take a step back from the limelight. And Jessie had quite enough going on in her life; her sister's praise and warmth had come at just the right time, and cast her in a light she was all too often denied.

Indeed, given that sibling rivalry can sometimes be even stronger than competition elsewhere, Jessie came across particularly well. To inspire such devotion in a younger family member showed she was doing something right. In fact, the entire family was a close one, watching out for one another and helping to pick up the pieces when something went wrong. It all helped when any of them came up against the problems and aggravations of this world.

As for Jessie, she had come through yet another difficult episode and was now preparing for imminent motherhood. Nothing if not resilient, she was, as ever, rising above it and taking the longer view. Her relationship with Dave might have been over and she had certainly suffered at the hand of his friend but, as ever, Jessie was getting on with her life. All that mattered now was the life-changing event that lay ahead. She had plenty to look forward to, and she focused all her energies on the most important and challenging task of her life: preparing for her baby's arrival. Everything else could be put on hold.

12

Over the Moon

As the time approached for Jessie to give birth, it initially seemed as if she and Dave were back on track. Her stay in hospital had resulted in a new and shared bond between them, which seemed as if it might really last. Dave attended to her the whole time throughout her stay there and could not have been more caring and more protective of his heavily pregnant fiancée. 'It was like starting over again,' said Jessie, after she'd come out. 'We've grown even closer. Whenever the time came for Dave to leave at the end of a hospital visit, I wouldn't want him to go. We're very happy. Dave will make a great dad.'

And, of course, the two were utterly delighted about the impending new arrival. Given that they had got engaged before the baby's presence was known, they clearly felt a great commitment towards each other and the future. The relationship had certainly been volatile at times, but now there was a period of real calm, of a sense of what was to lie ahead. In many ways, they were happier than they had ever been. It seemed that they had lots of good times to look forward to.

Jessie's friends were also relieved that the romance appeared to be back on track. 'He's been a tower of strength to her – unbelievably supportive throughout her pregnancy,' said one. 'And he's made it clear he wants to be a hands-on dad. We all hoped that they would get back together because they make such a really great couple.'

Certainly, the couple seemed to be as blissful as ever, if not more so. They were pictured together constantly, with Dave acting as Jessie's protector wherever they went. All rows and problems seemed to be in the past.

Meanwhile, Jessie was also drawing close to a break from the *EastEnders'* set. Her bosses had actually proved extremely accommodating; the last scenes she filmed were shot from the neck up, to conceal the fact that Jessie was very obviously on the verge of having a child. There had been no problems about writing her out of the script for a while – indeed, *EastEnders* was extremely keen to be as helpful as possible, because they had plans for her return.

And Jessie herself was coping well. She appeared at

the National Television Awards in late October, where she and Shane Richie were to present an award together. By common consent, Jessie was looking in vibrant health, while Shane brandished a rubber glove and informed the audience that he was ready if she started to go into labour there and then. She was even being quite relaxed about her career. 'I haven't really thought much about working,' she said, when asked at the ceremony about her future plans. 'I do want to go back, though. I love it and couldn't think of a better job.'

Indeed, Shane was one of the first to visit Jessie once she started her maternity leave. It had been agreed that she would have four months off, not a year, as had been previously reported, and she started her time off in the last weeks of her pregnancy.

According to Shane, she was being very well looked after. 'She phoned up the other day and said, "Shane! Can you bring me some more DVDs?" I said, "What happened to the pile I gave you last week?" And she said, "I've watched them all now, I'm bored." There's Dave looking after her like a princess while she puts her feet up and then she's got me popping round with DVDs for her to watch. It's like she's got two men in her life at the moment. And she's making my girlfriend Christie broody. We go round to see her and Dave, and she's saying to Christie, "You'll be next." She's a terrible influence!' She was also extremely happy and looking forward to the birth.

As her due date approached, Jessie still managed to make some television appearances, including going on Paul O'Grady's chat show as a guest, during which, like Shane, he joked that he was ready to help – this time with hot water and towels – if the baby arrived. What neither Paul himself nor the audience realised was that Jessie actually thought she might have gone into labour as she was appearing on the show, something she managed to conceal.

'It turned out to be a false alarm – what doctors call Braxton Hicks contractions,' she said afterwards. 'But it was pretty scary at the time. Afterwards, I told Paul what had happened and his jaw nearly hit the floor. At the time, I didn't know what was going on, but I just couldn't get comfortable. Whichever position I sat in, the pains just carried on.' It is a sign of Jessie's professionalism that no one had a clue that any of this was happening.

But Jessie was certainly ready for the new arrival. 'The nursery's ready, my bag is packed and I've got new jim-jams – so I'm all set,' she said. 'I can't wait. I'm not scared about the pain or nervous. I'm just really, really excited. I can feel the baby's bum sticking out and I love to stroke it. But when someone else does it, the baby moves, so it must know I'm its mum.'

Actually, Paul's suggestion that labour could happen

at any moment wasn't so far off. One week later, on 2 November 2004, a week earlier than expected, Jessie arrived at the Portland Hospital at 8.15am and, at 12.58pm, gave birth to her first child. It was a little girl and Dave was present throughout. 'Dave was floating around like a hovercraft,' a hospital source confided. 'He looked absolutely delighted, well over the moon.'

The press, of course, were in attendance and spoke to Dave as he left very briefly to buy a bunch of flowers. 'I'm a very proud dad,' he said, as it emerged that the baby, who weighed in at seven pounds fourteen ounces, was to be called Tallulah Lilac. 'She's very tired. There were no complications.' The couple were, in fact, absolutely thrilled – their little girl had finally arrived.

Of course, there was a great deal of speculation over what made Jessie choose the name Tallulah – it was said that she named her first child after Tallulah Bankhead, the 1920s star who most certainly knew how to party. And now that the new arrival was safely in her arms, Jessie was quite beside herself at the wonder of it all.

'I've never had a maternal bone in my body,' she said. 'My sister has five kids, but it didn't make me want to have them. But now I just want to be a baby machine – it's the most amazing feeling in the world, I can't wait to have more. I'd happily have another one right now if I could. I want lots of kids.'

Indeed, so besotted was she with her daughter that she

could hardly bear to be parted from her. Talking at a showbiz party that she attended with Dave a few weeks after Tallulah was born, Jessie could hardly think about anything else. 'I've never known anything like this before,' she said. 'We left Tallulah – or Lula as we call her – with friends, but I can't stop thinking about her. Tallulah has my big mouth… the poor thing. But she has Dave's eyes. I can't wait to get back to her. It's the most fantastic thing that's ever happened to me.'

It had completely changed her life. 'I've been reading *The Baby Whisperer*, which is all about how to bond with your baby,' Jessie said at the beginning of 2005. 'I started it when we went to Blackpool recently to see some friends. Tallulah wasn't with us and I just burst into tears on the plane – I missed her so much. Dave told me to put the book away. I don't really go into a deep sleep any more either as I'm always listening out for Tallulah. She is still sleeping in our room.

'She doesn't cry, though. All she does is gurgle during the night. I got out of bed last night when she woke up and she just laughed as if to say, "I made you come over to check on me!" I love playing with Lula's toys when she's asleep. She had loads of Christmas presents. She has a mat with toys hanging above it and I love to lie underneath it, looking at them. I think my brain has turned into mush!'

This is a far cry from the wild Jessie of old. She was

still going out and attending parties, but rather than wanting to be the life and soul from dusk 'til dawn, she now preferred to get home to see her baby. It was quite a turn up for the books. All talk was of Tallulah, of how she was getting on, what she was doing and any particularly entertaining developments she had made. And while Jessie might have said that her sister's children had not made her feel maternal as such, they had certainly given her some practice when it came to looking after one of her own.

It was also the first time since her meteoric rise to fame that she had actually taken any length of time out for herself. There had been holidays away, and that unfortunate period when she was suspended, which was so miserable it certainly couldn't have been any kind of a break, but ever since she had first joined the cast of *EastEnders*, the absolute focus of Jessie's life had been her work: nothing and no one had been allowed to come between it and her.

So determined had Jessie been to make up for all those lost years when she drifted, that she had devoted a huge amount of time and energy into making sure her career was going according to plan. Now, for the first time in years, it was not foremost in her mind. She was utterly preoccupied in something, or rather, someone, else.

And her happiness was really touching. Most new

mothers are overwhelmed with intense feelings for their new child, and Jessie was no exception; she really could scarcely talk about anything else. Her family was pretty delighted, too. Danielle, who was making a stir in the modelling world, was thrilled. 'I've never seen Jessie so happy,' she said. 'I saw Tallulah the day after she was born. I went to the Portland Hospital with my mum and other sister Joanne, with lots of presents for the baby. She is beautiful! Jessie was beaming – it's the happiest I've ever seen her. She's discovered that she is very maternal. Dave is looking after Jessie and Tallulah at the moment, but when he returns to work, I'm going to help out. I'm really looking forward to it.'

It was a happy time for all concerned but, in the background, there was Jessie's long-term future as one of Britain's favourite television stars to consider. Besotted with her daughter as she was, she had not become one of the nation's best-loved actresses for nothing, and she had every intention of returning to the programme that had made her name. And so, from fairly early on, she was aware that staying at home looking after Tallulah was very much a temporary state of affairs. Her daughter had enriched her life immeasurably, but she still wanted to return to work when the time was right. And so she took that on board and behaved accordingly, right from the start.

To begin with, of course, the ever-present pressure

to look good was still there, and Jessie was aware of it, too. 'I'm not breastfeeding, as I think it's anti-social,' she said. 'Anyway, my boobs are round my ankles. I have a running machine but all I do is look at it. I am eating sensibly but I'm not on a diet. I couldn't do anything like Atkins. You can't drink on that, can you?'

She was, however, looking forward to a return to the day job. 'I can't wait to go back to *EastEnders*,' she said. 'I start filming at the end of February. I really miss being there and all the people. I miss learning my lines. I am going to bring Tallulah with me to work. Kacey [Ainsworth] brings her daughter Blossom in as well, so they can play together. I'm so looking forward to getting back into it. It will be fantastic.'

As far as her relationship was concerned, though, Jessie was happy to let the situation rest as it was. She and Dave were still engaged, but she seemed in no hurry at all to formalise the union, with some reports saying she wanted to regain her figure before she walked down the aisle. Whatever the reason, the marriage itself was still some way away, with no sense of urgency that it should now take place.

'Dave and I have no plans to marry yet,' Jessie said. 'We are too busy with the baby now. He is such a great dad. He is used to crazy sleeping patterns as he is a fireman. Dave and I have a rota… we take it in turns to feed her and to get up during the night. And he doesn't mind changing her nappies at all. When it's your own baby, it's different.' Again, it was a sign that the couple seemed closer than they had ever been.

Meanwhile, Danielle was also getting used to the showbusiness world. She had found most people she encountered very welcoming – with the exception of Abi Titmuss. 'I've only been doing glamour modelling for about three months and everyone I've met has been fantastic,' she said. 'Lucy Pinder, Michelle Marsh and Jo Hicks have all been giving me tips. They've really welcomed me into their world.

'Abi is different. For some reason she just doesn't like me. She was someone I was really looking forward to meeting as I admire the way she's carved out a career for herself. But after meeting her a few times, I have to say I don't like her. She really needs to sort out her attitude. She's just so rude. I don't know whether it's because I am new to the glamour world or maybe she is threatened by me.'

But, unlike Abi, Danielle had not allowed her boyfriends to film their romps. 'I would never let anyone do that,' she said. 'But I love sex and I'm always keen to try out new things. I'm quite raunchy and love to dress up. One of my boyfriends bought me a skin-tight rubber cat suit with matching mask, which went down really well – He couldn't get enough of me! But the most exciting sex I've had was on a high-speed train. It was fantastic. No one knew what we were up to and the fact that we could get caught really turned me on.'

It emerged that Jessie had helped Danielle begin to make her way by introducing her to Dave Read, who had previously managed Jordan. Danielle had also had some past experience of showbiz, acting as Kate Hudson's body double in *The Four Feathers*. She had also appeared as a backing dancer in a video for pop group All Stars and had taken part in a Woolworth's advert alongside Ant and Dec.

'I am really excited but, at the same time, I'm pretty nervous,' said Danielle. 'It's all been going well so far and I know that if I work hard there's no reason why I can't be the next Jordan. She is someone I've always looked up to. I admire her success and how well she's done.'

Danielle had even been linked with Jordan's ex-boyfriend Scott Sullivan, but she denied it. 'Scott is a lovely lad but I've been single since splitting up with my last boyfriend six months ago,' she said. 'It's quite hard at times but now I'm just trying to concentrate on my career.'

Danielle was certainly becoming an increasingly public figure in her own right, although, of course, the intensity of the interest in her was fuelled by her famous sister. And so it was only natural that the press should have asked her point of view about the forthcoming marriage of Jessie and Dave, something that was still very much on the cards at the time. No date had been set, but neither had anything been put off for good. It seemed, back then, at least, that staging the actual ceremony was just a matter of time.

The two were bonding over their baby more strongly than ever, and so it seemed the most obvious step in the world to start thinking about their wedding plans. On top of that, Danielle was actually down to be a bridesmaid. 'Jessie is very happy,' she said. 'It's something she's dreamed about ever since she was a little girl. A wedding is one of the most exciting days of a woman's life. Jessie knew Dave was the one for her since they first met.' Jessie herself seemed thrilled at the idea. 'My fantasy revolves round an old church decked with fairy lights, a simple lace dress and wild flowers,' she said.

A friend gave an insight into what the couple wanted to do. 'There isn't an exact date yet, but it's definitely going to be in late summer,' she said. 'Jessie has this vision of a beautiful tented reception on a summer's night, where she and her family can celebrate under the stars. Having it in the summer also gives her time to lose the weight she put on while pregnant with Tallulah. She really wants to be a size 12 at the most when she walks down that aisle. Having been at home looking after Tallulah, Jessie's had time to look through some wedding magazines. It's really cute – she has an envelope stuffed with dress ideas and little things she's been inspired by.'

As for the honeymoon, Jessie and Dave, of course, now had someone else to take into consideration. 'She's a bit scared of travelling a long way with Tallulah and wouldn't want to be apart from her for more than a couple of days,' said a member of her circle. 'It's probably going to be somewhere with a flight time of less than eight hours. One of our friends went to Dubai with their young kids a while ago and they loved it – Jessie liked that suggestion.'

But behind the scenes, yet again, there was trouble brewing. The initial euphoria of having a baby had, perhaps, masked the couple's more deep-rooted problems but, as Jessie started to settle into the role of mother, flaws in the relationship began to surface again. Rows began and, although they were at first hidden from the public, it was becoming increasingly obvious that something was wrong.

Finally, as the time became near for Jessie to return to work, problems really set in. After a major bust-up, which came about after Jessie had a short holiday abroad, Dave left their shared home and, at times, was even seen sleeping in his car.

And, as ever with Jessie and Dave's relationship, it was all or nothing. One minute they were deliriously happy together, the next it was all over bar the shouting, and there seemed to be an awful lot of that. As they freely admitted themselves, they had always had a turbulent relationship, but this, alas, was different. The row escalated in its intensity, with the two going straight from domestic bliss to savage fighting. It was not a happy time.

'It's all a real mess at the moment,' said a friend. 'Dave and Jessie had a humdinger of a row and some terrible, hurtful things were said. Since then, Dave seems to have more or less moved out and has been kipping in his car or staying over at the station. He's still going home to see the baby, but things are obviously very strained and he looks terrible. He and Jessie have always had a volatile relationship – they admit that – but Tallulah's birth seemed to have drawn them close again. Now this has happened and it all looks pretty rocky again.'

Something had gone seriously wrong and onlookers were puzzled by the car business. After all, Dave had plenty of other places to go – why settle for such discomfort? One person actually observed his unusual sleeping arrangements. Dave had left his fire station and driven to a street overlooking Tower Bridge, where he spent the night. It seemed as if he was making some kind of a point, and he was certainly doing so very publicly.

'He was wearing a big padded jacket, jeans, boots and a baseball cap and seemed quite bulky as if he had several layers on,' said the source. 'Soon after arriving, he got out of the car and went to look in the window of an estate agent's that was advertising properties. But he quickly got back in the car as it was snowing and bitterly cold. It hit minus 2°C.

'He reclined the driver's seat as far as it would go, pulled his cap down over his eyes and went to sleep. He must have had the engine ticking over and the heating on as the snow was coming down really hard but didn't settle on the car. I couldn't believe how he could sleep like that, but he seemed to crash out and didn't stir until 6.30am.'

Some people believed that this behaviour was actually a plea to get Jessie to relent and start the relationship up again. 'Jessie has taken the decision to end the relationship for now and have a break,' said a source close to the couple. 'But they are determined to remain friends for the sake of Tallulah and continue to share parenting responsibilities. Only time will tell if they get back together. For now, they are apart.'

Others speculated on Dave's sleeping arrangements, too. 'It seems strange,' said another source. 'Maybe he is trying to gain sympathy. After all, he has many places he could stay with friends and family in central London. It's almost like he wants to appear the martyr.' If he did, this probably wasn't the best way to go about it. Jessie had a child to worry about now, and was unlikely to be impressed by dramatic gestures just for their own sake.

In total, Dave actually spent four nights sleeping in his car, going back to see Tallulah, but using the station to shower and look after himself. And then, as so often in their relationship, there was a brief reconciliation. From being on the verge of splitting, if not already split, Jessie and Dave were suddenly an item again. Indeed, events were moving so rapidly even their own friends were having trouble keeping up.

Dave himself was adamant that it had been a small incident that had blown up out of all proportion. 'It was just an argument,' he said. 'Jessie and I are both very happy, especially now Tallulah is here. We're not cancelling or anything outrageous like that. We're still very much in love.' He moved back in again, his nights in the car were history, and the relationship seemed to be back on track.

But it didn't last long. Shortly afterwards, there was another major bust-up, and this time it was for good. The relationship was just too volatile, it seemed, and Jessie simply couldn't take any more. And, eventually, she was forced to issue a statement to end all the speculation. It was made quite clear that the relationship was finally at an end. 'Jessie Wallace is saddened to announce her relationship with partner Dave Morgan, who is the father of their daughter Tallulah, is at an end and they have separated,' it said.

'I've had enough of all the rows,' she was said to have told a friend. 'It's not good for the baby. I've tried to make things work time and again, but it's not meant to be. In the past, I've always gone back to Dave because it's scary being on your own with a young child. But now I'm confident I can be happy on my own. Everyone told me Dave wasn't right for me, but I kept hoping things would get better. Now I know there's no point staying together. I'm better off alone. He and I are still friends and our first priority's Tallulah.' This time it really was the last time. Jessie was a free woman – and it was time for her to go back to work again.

13

Back to Square One

It was not what she wanted or expected; with a five-month baby girl, Jessie was single, with no wedding plans and no partner to rely on. At that point, she thought she still had Dave's support, although matters between them were soon to turn so hostile that she could not rely on that either. This had not been the future Jessie was thinking of when she was first whisked away by Dave in his police car to safety, and the joys of new-found love.

'It's heartbreaking for all of us,' Jessie said. 'But it's better that Tallulah is brought up in a happy household rather than having her parents at each other's throats. We've tried very hard to make our relationship a success but, when it came to the crunch, we realised we just weren't suited. We've been arguing a lot. We never had the easiest of relationships and, of course, I'm very sad it's over, but we've come to the end of the road.'

Even so, she was coping well. Always a strong character, she seemed to thrive in adversity, and this unexpected problem just made her all the more determined to get on with her life and carve out a future for herself and her daughter. And it cleared something else up, too. There had been some speculation that she might not want to return to *EastEnders* now that she had a child but this was quite emphatically not the case. In April 2005, she signed a £200,000 deal to continue with the show for now – an action for which her BBC bosses rewarded her by taking her out to The Ivy – and signalled her determination to return to where she belonged.

'Jessie feels she's better off at this time keeping busy,' said a friend. 'She considered quitting, but things have gone pretty well and bosses are really pleased to have her back in the fold. They made Jessie feel wanted and really special; she had a change of heart and decided to stay. The money she was being offered was too good to refuse, especially as she faces life as a single mum.'

Life as a single mother was not all she had to worry about, however. There was a rather ominous sign of what was to come when Jessie called her lawyers in to talk about the split. And it soon emerged that what had really caused her to call the relationship off for good was that Dave was said to be planning to sell a piece to a magazine about the life the two led.

'This was the final straw in what's been a turbulent relationship,' said a source. 'Jessie guards her privacy jealously. She's had suspicions about people close to her selling stories before, and told Dave she considered it a breach of confidence. He was about to sign up for a positive glossy mag piece about their happy family life and wedding plans. But when she found out, she was fuming. He went on the defensive and said if he had wanted to stitch her up, he had had plenty of opportunities before now. Understandably, that didn't go down well. Jessie kicked him out and told him that it was over for good this time.'

What Dave finally did end up doing, though, was considerably worse. He sold a kiss-and-tell story that went into great detail about their lives together, starting with the fact that Jessie was keen on his fireman's uniform. 'I'd briefly worked over in New York for their fire service and brought my uniform back – Jessie loved it,' he said. 'It's so much sexier than the British firefighting gear.'

Dave also maintained that Jessie was extremely keen to have a child. 'I think Jessie was aware her biological clock was ticking,' he said. 'We tried for three or four months and she started getting really worried. Then it happened and we were obviously thrilled.'

Unfortunately, however, their love life suffered. 'Jessie just wasn't interested in it while she was pregnant,' said Dave. 'Even after she'd had the baby, she wasn't interested. Before we split last month, we hadn't made love for two months at least. By then, we were rowing so much that I spent a lot of the time in the spare room.'

Jessie was also very jealous, according to Dave. 'Jessie and me had been out with this couple called Steve and Lisa a couple of times but didn't really know them that well,' said Dave. 'One day, in passing, I happened to mention that they'd split up and Jessie gave me an odd look. Then, when I was in New York, she got on the phone to Lisa and accused her of having an affair with me, apparently effing and blinding down the phone at her. It was all nonsense, of course.

'When I found out, I had a go at her about it and we ended up having another flaming row. She'd ask me if it bothered me when she kissed Shane. I'd say it didn't, but when I said it must be nasty snogging someone else, she just shrugged and said, "It's work, isn't it?"'

There was a great deal more along these lines – tales of jealousy, drinking and physical violence. One story had it that Jessie gave up breastfeeding so that she could drink alcohol, and another had her physically attacking Dave. But this time, Dave had gone too far. Jessie was, after all, the mother of his child and, no matter how he was feeling, this was simply beyond the pale. Indeed, the row, which was already nasty enough, soon turned even worse.

For a start, Jessie could scarcely believe what he had done. 'How could anyone do this to the mother of his child?' she asked. 'He is a parasite who sponged off me. He's evil and I hate him! How dare he suggest I'm an unfit mother? It is outrageous. I love Tallulah more than anything and would never do anything to put her at risk. I cannot believe he has done this. It is the lowest of the low.' Lawyers were called in, both to try to stop further revelations and to work out what would happen about their child.

Her friends rallied round, both appalled at Dave's behaviour and relieved he was out of her life. 'Last week, she had to endure so many calls from Dave. In their two years together, she must have spent at least £100,000 on him. She splashed out on luxury cars, holidays to the Maldives and New York. It's highly unlikely they'll have to meet. It will most likely just go through lawyers and Jessie really wants to maintain her dignity. She's not even sure yet how much involvement Dave wants with Tallulah.'

Dave certainly didn't appear to have thought through the longer-term consequences of his actions. All the signs were that Jessie had dumped him, something he denied, and he was lashing out like a scorned lover, but he still didn't seem to understand the impact this would have on his child, let alone the long-term relationship with Tallulah's mother. 'She is deeply hurt by what Dave has done and has been in tears,' said a friend. 'She can't believe he has stooped so low and effectively ruined any chance of a friendship with the mother of his child. How will Tallulah feel when she grows up and realises what her dad did to her mum?

'He isn't thinking about the long-term consequences of his relationship with his daughter. Jessie would never ban him from seeing Tallulah, but she is so angry at the moment she doesn't want anything to do with him. There are a number of allegations that are simply wrong and to suggest Jessie is an unfit mother is utterly reprehensible. Anyone who knows her knows that Tallulah is everything to her. There are many professional women who enjoy a drink after a hard day at work but to suggest that Jessie is regularly out on the tiles, leaving Tallulah at home, is rubbish.'

Could it get any nastier? Yes. Not only had Jessie dumped Dave, rather than the other way around, but there were claims that it was he, not she, who had threatened physical violence. Dave did not take this lying down. 'If she wants to play that game, I'm ready,' he raged in a phone call to a national newspaper. 'I've got so much more on her, believe me. I have got so much more to say and, if it's going to get nasty, I'm game on. I'll ruin her! I don't adhere to violence against women — it's complete rubbish.' It was becoming the stuff of nightmares.

Of course, Jessie and Dave had had rows and break-ups before, but nothing like this one. Dave continued to lash out, threatening to make yet more accusations, while her friends continued to make it clear just what they thought of him. Those nights spent sleeping in his car were written off as childish posturing, and there were repeated mutterings about how it was Jessie who had funded their lifestyle together. It was a very sad end to what had once seemed to promise so much, but it must be said that whatever the faults on either side, it was Dave who had completely destroyed any possibility of building bridges again.

Jessie, trooper that she is, coped. 'Everyone has been really supportive of me. I've got my friends and family — it's made me a stronger person. I've got my baby to think of, she's in the middle of this. I've got her needs to think of, and that's that. I have a handful of really close friends. Along with my family, they really know me. They're there for me and that's all I need now.'

Indeed, so shaken was she by what had happened that she was even talking about making a complete change in her life. 'I want to be in the countryside,' said Jessie. 'I really want to get out of the city. I really also want to be somewhere there are good schools. I've never been so organised. Tallulah's completely changed my life; she's all I think of. My priorities have definitely changed now. It's all about her now. At the moment, I'm just taking life one step at a time.'

As fate would have it, the person who actually ended up in the countryside was none other than Dave. He had been signed up to *The Farm*, the reality show best known for featuring Rebecca Loos pleasuring a pig, and there was much salivation on all sides as to what he would come up with next. 'Dave is clearly an angry man,' said one rather over-excited commentator. 'What better way to put the knife in than appearing on a prime-time telly programme with a bunch of celebs dying to know what Jessie is really like?'

In the event, the celebs, and the very few viewers who tuned in, were to be disappointed. Showing a certain lack of understanding over what he had just done, far from dissing Jessie on live TV, Dave appeared to be attempting to get her back. 'Stuck in here for a couple of weeks might help sort it out,' he said, displaying a rather misguided optimism. 'Hopefully, fingers crossed, it'll all get sorted out eventually. I miss my little girl… she might be crawling by the time I get out. I still miss them both, I miss them loads – I really do. It's a shame, really. If you have a break-up in the public eye, everyone wants to know about it. It really is a shame. I still love her and stuff, you know. I'd go back tomorrow if she said, "Go back." If you hate someone, it's easier to get over, but I don't hate her at all.'

If truth be told, this behaviour was bordering on the bizarre. Possibly, Dave had had time to calm down; possibly, it was only just beginning to occur to him what he had done. But to expect Jessie to take him back after all of this would have been unrealistic in the extreme.

At any rate, he did finally appear to accept that matters had got out of hand. Jessie had gone to the High Court to seek a ban to silence Dave, and he finally came round to this, giving her a binding promise that he would not talk any more about their life together. The couple, according to Jessie's solicitor Simon Smith, had agreed not to publish 'personal, private or confidential information' about their life without 'mediation'.

However, in case anyone should take that to mean that bridges were to be built, he added that the proposed mediation was 'not with a view to reconciliation', but 'with a view to see who can say what in the future'. It was, at least, a weight off her mind, for Jessie was not only having to cope with the anger of an ex-lover, but with being a single mother, too. And, as she was finding out, it was exhausting.

'When I get home, I don't learn my lines for the next day as I'm busy with Tallulah,' she said. 'Instead, I set the alarm for 4.00am and do it then. I've been getting about four hours' sleep recently as I can't relax properly, but your body gets used to it, I guess. I've stopped exercising because I'm too tired to do it. I did get bored with it. I feel like I've put on a bit of weight recently. The last few weeks I've been pigging out. I didn't have a personal trainer, I couldn't cope with that – I don't want someone screaming at me.'

What she actually got was something quite different – support from people she had known long ago in her past. There had been widespread sympathy for Jessie after what Dave had done, and not only from her close friends and family. Other people in showbusiness were not very impressed and neither, it seemed, were past acquaintances who had known her many years previously. Dave had painted Jessie as a foul-mouthed drinker with a violent streak. A totally different picture now emerged from people she had known years earlier during her seven-month stint in Portugal.

'She was a very quiet girl,' said a friend, who had known her at the time. 'You wouldn't believe the difference now. Remembering the girl I knew then, I can't imagine how she built up the confidence to go in front of the cameras for *EastEnders*. A lot of us did karaoke in the bars, but she was too shy. She would never go up and sing on her own. We had great times out there. Everyone stuck together. We'd all meet up in the evenings after work and drink until the early hours.

At the end of the season, we were all really close – one big family, including Jessie. She was like our kid sister.'

It was certainly a long way from the Jessie that Dave portrayed, and it revealed a much happier time than Jessie had talked about in the past. She was certainly frightened at times and, ultimately, became desperate to get back to England, but at the same time Portugal was a big experience for her. For the first time in her life, she was on her own, and she had to make it work. For this was also an experience that finally made her decide, once and for all, to make something of her life. It could almost be said to be responsible for her ending up in *EastEnders*.

'When you're working abroad, it's a bit of an education,' said the friend. 'You're meeting different people all the time from all over the world. I think Jessie found it a bit of a confidence-builder. She was always more confident after a few drinks once she was relaxed. A couple of times, she went up to sing with a group of girls, but that was only after a couple of drinks.'

Even so, Jessie was no pushover. She might have been a shy young thing, and a long way removed from the confident actress of today, but she was still capable of making her presence felt. 'She would always speak her mind,' said her friend. 'If she wasn't happy about something, she would put you straight, but we all really liked her. We can't recognise what Dave Morgan says about her. It's like he's talking about a different girl. She did bar work in a couple of pubs and restaurant-bars and everyone was always happy with her because she worked hard. She moved in with a group of girls after a while but was still a lot quieter than the rest of them.'

Indeed, they all became a little ex-pat community, enjoying the beautiful weather and the opportunities available in the Algarve. Real friendships were forged and bonds made. Everyone was young and just wanted to have fun – which they did. It was all innocent and rather charming. 'Every Saturday we played sport,' said her friend. 'There was a Superstars competition over the eleven weeks of summer. One week it was running 800 metres, next week swimming, the week after that shooting or something else. Jessie would come to cheer us along and gave out some of the awards at the end of the season. She never really talked about home. We always thought it was because her family were going through a tough time.

'There were about ten of us who were really close, but because Jessie was a quiet girl she was the last one I expected to become famous. She never mentioned wanting to be famous or talked about becoming an actress. I've run into her a few times and she always says hello and we have a laugh about the old times.' This was a Jessie capable of making and maintaining friendships, and one who had not dropped her old friends because of her new-found fame.

There was another rather enormous consolation to hand as well: Tallulah. Jessie was utterly besotted with her daughter and could hardly stop talking about her. Becoming a mother changes most people and that certainly seemed to be the case with her; her baby was now, beyond shadow of doubt, her priority. 'All my friends say, "You're not as selfish as you used to be,"' she said. 'No one can tell you until you have your baby how strongly you're going to feel. Lulah is all I think about... she comes before anything.

'She's got a real character. She looks people up and down and gives them dirty looks. And she absolutely loves the Crazy Frog TV advert. Her arms start flapping when it comes on. I sing the tune to her and she goes mad so I've constantly got the song going around in my head.'

Given the amount of attention Jessie had had to put up with, however, she was a very protective mother. It was not just the recent spat with Dave that had focused her mind; she had had to deal with the interest of the public and the press practically from the word go, and she was determined that Tallulah would not have to do the same. 'I made a pact with myself when she was born to keep her out of the spotlight,' she said. 'When we came out of the hospital, there were about thirty

photographers and I didn't want to expose her face to all
the flashes. Someone said I was trying to hide her face
because I had a big deal with a magazine, which was not
true. It's my choice if I want my picture taken – well,
sometimes – but it's not hers, and I'll try my hardest to
protect her from that.'

And, like any new mother, Jessie was nervous about
looking after her little girl. 'I was terrified when I
brought her home from the hospital,' she said. 'It took
a little while then it all just fell into place. Funny, when
I first went to wind her I didn't know what I was doing
– I was so cack-handed. Now it's just natural.'

She was taking to it like a duck to water. However,
there had been other, more fundamental changes to
Jessie, too. Indeed, she seemed to have gained a deeper
level of maturity from what had happened, and was sad
that Tallulah, like Jessie herself, would have to grow up
in a broken home.

'I will do whatever I can to protect my little girl,' she
said. 'No one wants that for their child, no one. But
because I've been through it, I know exactly what her
needs are going to be. I just take things one day at a
time. You never know what's around the corner and I'm
enjoying being with my baby.'

She had also decided to be a lot more careful when it
came to choosing boyfriends. It was one thing to run
around town enjoying herself when she was single, but

now that she had a baby, everything had changed. Any man she met would not just be dealing with Jessie, after all, but with Tallulah, too, and she was determined that her daughter would not watch a string of men wandering in and out of her life.

'I won't do that to her,' she said. 'I could bring someone into her life and perhaps separate with that person. It's just not fair to her – she's my first priority. In the past, I haven't been a great judge of character, I know that. But now I don't trust anyone easily. I can't, because I have Tallulah to think about. I can't go letting just anyone into her life: I have to protect her.'

The split with Dave had certainly taken its toll. It really was an awful betrayal and Jessie wouldn't have been human if she hadn't been upset about it. As it was, she could still scarcely believe what he'd done. 'It has been so difficult,' she said. 'But the way I look at it is that I've had so much to put up with, I've reached rock bottom. I've been at the point where I couldn't get much lower, so everything else just piles on. I can take it now – there's something in me that's got a lot stronger. It would have been a lot harder if I didn't have Tallulah.'

It helped that her long-awaited return to Albert Square was finally going to take place, and a very emotional time it was, too. 'The very first scene I filmed was walking back into the pub with Alfie and I'm just so glad all I had to say was, "Hello," because I don't think I'd have been able to say any more,' Jessie said. 'I had worked myself up and was a bag of nerves. It was brilliant being reunited with Kat's slap. As soon as I started to put her clothes on, I started to mince! I have missed dressing up as Kat.'

Indeed, it felt like a return to old times. Her months away from the soap had been as full of incident as everything else in Jessie's life, and she now found that she had to get back into the swing of her role. 'I had to get back into the rhythm of Kat,' said Jessie. 'But as soon as I put that mini-skirt on and the lipstick, I thought, "She's back." I started mincing around. I was given a little clutch bag with a handle on it and I was holding it, but I said to Shane Richie, "I don't feel like Kat… I don't know what it is." So I tucked the handles in, stuck it under my arm and thought, "That's it… now I'm Kat."'

Her reappearance in the Square was, of course, as dramatic as could be expected, given Kat's turbulent life to date. Kat, it emerged, had been in prison (for assaulting a policeman – quite a few people felt the screenwriters were having their own little joke) and ended up in a hostel with no money. Big Mo discovers that Kat is behind bars, and at first decides to say nothing.

'She keeps quiet about her secret discovery but tracks Kat down on Tuesday after learning she's been released and is at a hostel,' said a spokesman for *EastEnders*. 'She's quite shocked at the change in Kat and how much more hardened she has become, but cannot persuade her to return to the Slater fold.'

Fortunately, however, for the programme and for Kat fans everywhere, matters promptly take a turn for the worse. 'She decides against going back to Walford and goes to stay at a hostel while she finds somewhere permanent to live,' said the spokesman. 'But someone steals her money from her room and she is forced to leave. Things will take an even bigger downturn when she does get back to the Queen Vic – just as her sister Little Mo is about to decide to start seeing her estranged husband Alfie. But that's the sort of thing that could act as a spur for Kat to turn her life around.' It was pure *EastEnders*, and the viewers loved it.

Jessie loved it, too. 'I've got some brilliant storylines and some lovely new cast members,' she said. 'The vibe I get is people saying to me it'll be great to have Kat back, but I can't help thinking, "But what if I come back and people think I'm not that great?" It's like going back to your family – June Brown, Wendy Richard, Pam St Clement – all that lot. They are so welcoming. It's great being back with Shane Richie [Alfie Moon] again.

'A lot of people are rooting for Little Mo and Alfie. I'm sure I'm going to get a lot of hate mail from fans saying I'm bad for him and that Kat should leave them alone to get on with it. I think they're going to get back together, but I don't know how. She fights to get Alfie back. I've only been back a few months but I've already had about four punch-ups. We get really good stunt co-ordinators who show you how to throw a really good punch. I have never hit anyone in my life, though!'

Jessie did, however, find it a bit of a shock to be back on screen. 'I thought I looked OK but when I saw myself on the monitor the other day I thought, "Yuck, I look huge," she said. 'When I came out of hospital, I felt like I'd had implants. It was awful. My boobs were out there and were huge. And they were killing me. I put cabbage leaves on them but it made them smell like old farts! I would definitely have surgery on my breasts again. I'd have anything done. I don't think there's anything wrong with that whatsoever, so I don't have to rely on scaffolding!'

And now that she was back, she was defensive of her alma mater. *EastEnders* had been going through one of its periodic phases when everyone laid into it, and Jessie had been thoroughly irritated by the remarks. 'I feel very protective of the way people are laying into *EastEnders*,' she said. 'It's the same as any other soap. It has its ups and downs. At the end of the day, it's been going for twenty years and it's got brilliant characters. But I feel it's been picked on quite a lot and it's unfair.'

Delighted as she was to be back at work, though, there was no doubt who was the real focus of Jessie's life. Her baby meant everything to her and everyone was piling in to help; both her parents were helping to look after their grandchild and a nanny had been hired as well. Even so, Jessie could not wait to be back with her every evening.

'Tallulah is the love of my life,' she said. 'I can't imagine my life without her. It's such an unconditional love, it's an overwhelming feeling. She put her hand on my cheek last night and held my face. I wanted to cry. It's when she tells me she loves Mummy that'll be it for me.'

Jessie was really beginning to think about the future, though. Her time away from *EastEnders* had given her plenty to mull over, not least what to do next. And she was starting to think, at long last, that perhaps she would leave the show. After all, she had been on it for nearly five years, and new challenges were beckoning.

'I would love to do theatre,' she said. 'That's what it's all about for an actor – it's getting that buzz from the audience. I'd love to do the Royal Court in London. Not panto – I want to do good, decent plays. People would walk out if I did a musical, though. I once auditioned for *Whistle Down the Wind*. There were all these girls at the audition with floaty dresses and I went bulldozing in there with ripped jeans, a Diesel top and

Timberland boots. They asked me what I was going to sing so I said, "I've Got to Get Out of This Place" by the Animals. They were horrified. I really went for it, I was completely out of tune. They booted me straight out of the door.'

That good old self-deprecating sense of humour was certainly still in evidence. But Jessie had changed and, if anything proved it, it was her reaction when she was in a nightclub called Movida in the West End. Another woman started shouting at her, trying to provoke her. Jessie was having none of it and impressed everyone with the way she kept her calm.

'Jessie hadn't been out for ages and was letting her hair down for the first time in months,' said an onlooker. 'Since she split with Dave, she's been spending most of her nights reading scripts and playing with her daughter, Tallulah Lilac. She was having a great time with some mates in the club's VIP area and was the life and soul of the party. All of a sudden, her face dropped. She got the attention of one of the club's managers and said, "This girl really scares me. She's really aggressive towards me... Please keep her away from me." But when she got up to go to the VIP toilet, this woman ran straight after her. She collared Jessie outside the ladies and started speaking in raised tones.

'Her mannerisms were quite threatening and, although Jessie wasn't retaliating, you could tell she was intimidated. Several security guys rushed over to keep them apart before the situation got more heated and Jessie decided she wanted to leave immediately. The other girl was held behind in the club until Jessie had got safely into a car, to make sure she didn't start on her again. Jessie was completely blameless but the incident took the shine off what should have been a great night.'

It did, however, have an upside. Jessie had proved that she had learnt from past mistakes and could walk away from a potential fracas. She knew how to cope with her fame and deal with trouble in a controlled and sensible manner. She had started a whole new period in her life.

14

Pastures New

Even by Jessie's standards, it had been an incredibly turbulent year. The birth of Tallulah, the split with Dave, the return to *EastEnders*, to say nothing of the various dramas raging in the background... all had contributed to make this one of the most tumultuous periods of her life. And so it was inevitable that she would now take stock, and decide what to do next. She eventually made the decision her *EastEnders* bosses had been dreading – that it was time, at long last, to leave the show.

The decision, while brave, was one that had to be made. Some actors and actresses are content to spend many decades on the programme they have become associated with, but Jessie had always seen *EastEnders* as the launching pad to her career, not an ultimate end in itself. The break was going to have to be made at some point and, with so much change in her life, now was the right time to make the decision.

And there was another element at play; Shane Ritchie, who was equally keen to expand his repertoire, had also decided it was time to leave. It was a clear indication that times were about to change.

On top of that, while the *EastEnders* powers that be might not have been delighted, the BBC itself was adamant that she had a great future with the Corporation. Jessie would be leaving the programme, but not the channel that had made her name. 'It's really disappointing that Jessie is going, but she feels ready to move on,' said a BBC source. 'At least it looks like she's not leaving the BBC altogether.' And in another clear indication of support for their star, Jessie's character was to be written out in December 2005, but not killed off. There would be a way back if that's what she ultimately wanted.

There seemed to be a great deal of under-standing among the hierarchy at the BBC itself as to why Jessie wanted to make a move. Not only was she a talented actress, but her overnight leap to fame in one of the first roles she had ever played meant that she had not had the opportunity to experience other parts. She wanted to try her hand at something new and do some theatre work. It was, after all, while working in the

theatre as a make-up artist that she first got a taste of
the desire to act.

'Jessie is a real talent and it's great news that she'll be
staying at the BBC after *EastEnders*,' said another BBC
source. 'Kat has been a fantastic character, but Jessie
is ready for new challenges and the writers wanted her
to go out on a high. Jessie's interested in tackling roles
which are a million miles from Kat Slater – everything
from costume drama to comedy.'

She also had a very important ally – John Yorke.
John had been in charge of *EastEnders* in 2000, the year
the Slaters moved into the Square, and was now in
charge of drama at the BBC. It was he who, to all
intents and purposes, discovered Jessie, and he was
now very keen to promote her talents elsewhere. With
that kind of backing, Jessie was sure to be offered the
parts that would promote her abilities to the full and,
indeed, talk began to surface about the new projects
and dramas in which she would play a lead.

There was certainly plenty of goodwill from her
friends and fans at the BBC. In many ways, it was an
exciting time for all of them; not just Jessie, who was
going on to experience new, stimulating challenges, but
the executives who would be able to try her out in new
roles. 'The BBC have high hopes for Jessie and are
planning to a create a star vehicle in which to showcase
her talents,' said a BBC insider. 'There are lots of ideas

out there, but Jessie wants to make sure that what she is doing is absolutely right for her career. She hasn't made a final decision about what she wants to do yet, but it is pretty much guaranteed she will be starring in a drama series written with her in mind as the lead.' This was heady stuff. Jessie had taken her place in the extremely small pantheon of British television stars who have a real choice and degree of control about what they do.

And playing Kat had taken its toll. It had been a punishing schedule, and the demands of a long-running soap combined with a new baby were exhausting. Sleeping for an average of about four hours a night was not sufficient to enable Jessie to cope with the workload, so leaving *EastEnders'* at least held the promise of slightly more time to herself. Her mother Annette recognised this. 'Jessie has to cope with the demands of long days on the *EastEnders* set and the pressures of raising a young daughter on her own,' she said. 'It's not easy. She's devoted to Tallulah. I had dinner with her a couple of weeks ago and she seemed fine. But it's hard for her. She hasn't told me of any problems, though – Jessie keeps herself to herself.'

Jessie was also having to come to some agreement about how to settle matters with Dave. He was, after all, the father of her child, and so she couldn't refuse to see him ever again, no matter how much she might have wanted to. Instead, she allowed herself a moment of anger, in which she sold off all his belongings in a jumble sale, something she clearly found extremely therapeutic. The sale included an iPod, designer clothes, a laptop and motorbike leathers. 'She made the sale into a social event and was cackling like a witch all the way through it,' said a friend. 'Her mates got some real bargains and Jessie made quite a bit of cash. But Dave was really upset when he found out.'

However, Jessie also decided that the two really had to reach some kind of compromise. They decided to visit a mediator, who spoke about their 'shared goal' of coming to some kind of agreement. It seemed to help.

'They finally agreed to go to mediation earlier this month,' said a friend. 'It has been a long time coming, but Jessie finally decided that she and Dave had to come to an agreement for everyone's sake. They may have their personal issues, but they realised they had to put those to one side for the sake of Tallulah.' It was, at least, a start.

And Jessie had other issues to deal with as well. She was having some concerns about where she lived; she had already had to move once since becoming famous as Kat, and it looked as if she might be doing so again. Given her celebrity, she tended to become involved in neighbourhood disputes, even when none of them were anything to do with her.

'Jessie is furious after the latest row escalated with

one of the locals,' said a source. 'Just because she is so high profile, she seems to get dragged into all the area's disputes but there's nothing she can do – she only wishes she could. There is one particular "problem-creator", who is persistent with his nagging. He calls at Jessie's home at all hours and insists on calling her by her real name, Karen.

'He gossips with other people in the neighbourhood about the fact that there are always paparazzi waiting for her. So Jessie wants to move away to the countryside with seven-month-old daughter Tallulah. The local kids will be devastated when Jessie goes as she is so much part of the community. But her bickering neighbours will no doubt find something else to moan about.'

It was all taking its toll and some indication of the kind of stress Jessie was under came when a relatively trivial incident occurred – she lost her mobile phone. She was on the set of *EastEnders* when it happened and, by all accounts, became quite overwhelmed. She became so upset, in fact, that she actually had to go home. 'Jessie was sent home unwell on Thursday but turned up for work as normal on Friday,' an *EastEnders* spokesman said.

But it turned out to be a little more than that. Jessie seems to have had full-blown hysterics, becoming so overwrought that those around her were really quite concerned. 'Jessie got really upset when she couldn't find her mobile and got really worked up,' said someone who had witnessed the scene. 'She got more and more distraught. It got to the point where she was crying and had become so emotional they had to send her home in a car.' This could be taken as diva-like behaviour, but it was far more likely that Jessie was simply exhausted and, after all the strains of the previous year, sometimes found it hard to cope.

That said, her storylines on the show were as headline-grabbing as ever. Kat wasn't just back, she was making her presence felt with a vengeance — 'vengeance' being the operative word — and Jessie was loving every minute of it. The latest drama concerned her on-screen husband Alfie. Kat's belief that the two were happily reunited was blown to smithereens when she finally discovered that he had been courting her sister, Little Mo.

'The news causes real physical pain,' said Jessie, who was clearly relishing this extraordinarily juicy storyline. 'It is much more than a slap in the face — more like a punch in the head. One moment Kat has everything she had ever wanted, the next it's gone. Kat's heart sings when Alfie confides he wants her to move in and for them to start a family. She cries with joy.'

But the fly in the ointment was Billy. Having had a few in the Queen Vic, he grabs the microphone during a karaoke session and congratulates Alfie and Little Mo on their togetherness. This does not go down well and Kat takes matters into her own hands in the way that only she can. 'She lashes out at Little Mo and, for a moment, she really wants to hurt her,' said Jessie. 'She drags her sister out of the Vic. But it's a one-sided catfight because Little Mo doesn't really fight back. The sisters return home and Kat turns her fury on the kitchen, smashing the place up.'

It was all classic *EastEnders* stuff, complete with a declaration from Little Mo that while she and Alfie have never been intimate, her feelings for him are real. 'Kat just wants to punish everyone, including herself,' said Jessie. 'But then she realises how much Little Mo's suffered as well. She hates Alfie and when he comes round, she hurls a vase at him! She's glad when it hits him as she wants him to hurt as much as she does. Alfie almost talks her into getting back with him, but she's convinced it couldn't work. She can't do it to Little Mo. She is just numb with agony over the total mess of her life. She knows she's lost the only man she'll ever love.' In the end, to keep everyone guessing, the producers filmed two endings to the dilemma – one happy and one tragic.

Jessie's recent experiences gave a quality to her acting that really brought these scenes out. While it would be completely inaccurate to call Dave the love of her life, her experiences with him had still been bruising, giving an added depth to her personality and her acting that hadn't been there before. Just as it was always said that

Frank Sinatra became a better singer after he lost Ava Gardner, due to the amount of suffering it caused, so Jessie had been through a very rough time, which, perversely, made her a better actress still. It might not have felt like much consolation, but she was certainly able to use her recent past in her professional life.

And *EastEnders* itself was now going through one of its better times. The love triangle storylines kept the viewers gripped, while the writing was deemed to be as good as it ever had been. One line at the time – 'Billy, don't be a Mitchell,' – was particularly good. And although there was something of an exodus from Albert Square in the pipeline – alongside Jessie and Shane, Nigel Harman (Dennis Rickman) and Letitia Dean (Sharon Rickman) were also on the move – there were a couple of very much anticipated returns as well, in the form of the Mitchell brothers, Phil and Grant, aka Steve McFadden and Ross Kemp.

'The stories coming up for Christmas and New Year are just explosive,' said a spokeswoman for *EastEnders*. Kate Harwood, the executive producer of the show, was also delighted at what lay ahead. 'I can't wait for our viewers to see what we have got in store for the rest of the year,' she said. To cap it all, *EastEnders* then won Best Soap at the *Inside Soap* Awards. Everyone was pleased by the turn of events.

Everyone in Jessie's professional life, that is. Yet

again, matters blew up between her and Dave, this time over access to Tallulah and Jessie's feeling that Dave might let the press see his little girl. The problem, it seemed, arose because Dave had taken some pictures of her on her last visit.

'Jessie's extremely protective and thinks Dave will secretly allow Tallulah to be photographed for a magazine or something,' said a friend. 'She just doesn't trust him so she's totally gone back on the agreement. But Dave's furious. He thinks it's a bit rich when Jessie's been known to tip off photographers about her own movements in the past. He misses Tallulah desperately. He's only seen her twice since splitting with Jessie in April. It's tough – Tallulah's growing up fast and he's missing lots of key moments. Dave keeps frantically calling Jessie's family hoping they'll persuade her, but it's all falling on deaf ears.'

Of course, Dave couldn't really have expected anything else. Jessie was so upset at what he'd done that it was unsurprising that she was not ready to fall in easily with his plans. Her life had changed; she was no longer a soap star with a liking for a night on the tiles, but a mother and professional actress with an extremely promising career in front of her. She had made mistakes and was ready to admit to them. But, more than at any time in her life to date, Jessie was quite determined not to allow herself to be pushed around.

Epilogue

All in all, it's been a remarkable story. Jessie Wallace, from an unassuming background in North London, has become one of the biggest stars in Britain today. And the way she got there was quite extraordinary – from fooling around at school to drifting in her twenties, to life as a make-up artist, actress and then major star. And the secret of it all, of course, is that Jessie does have star quality. It is no coincidence that her off-screen life has been filled with almost as much incident as Kat's: she draws people to her. When she walks into a room, her presence is felt. Whatever you might think about Jessie Wallace, she is impossible to ignore and it is that which has made her stand out from the crowd.

All this and she's still in her early thirties. And so what

next? Professionally, the future looks very bright; she has the backing and confidence of the BBC, and is bound to want to try out a number of new ideas now that she has finally left Albert Square.

Despite the high drama that Kat's life has entailed, Jessie has yet to test her true range since she first appeared on *EastEnders* on the back of a milk float, swigging from a bottle of champagne. Musical comedy we may safely assume to be out of the question, but everything else is very much up for grabs. And there will be no shortage of offers now that she is a free woman again. What she decides to do next will be very much her own decision, but some experimentation is also likely. In the past Jessie has often spoken about how much she would like to do stage work, and now she will get the chance.

And her personal life? On the one hand, of course, with Tallulah, she has found complete fulfilment in motherhood and is almost bound to want more children in the future. Jessie seems personally softened by motherhood, although on screen she remains as sharp as ever. As for the men in her life, however, at the time of writing there was no one (publicly, at least) on the scene. There is no question that she wants to be more careful in the future; from boyfriends with dubious pasts to those who have sold her down the river, she has been a little bit unlucky with men.

But Jessie is a beautiful woman with her life ahead of her. She is very close to her friends and family and has inspired tremendous loyalty among those to whom she is close. She has managed to stay close to all her old friends, despite the kudos that stardom has brought her, and still, despite everything, has kept her feet on the ground.

And she now has a firmly established domestic set-up. She has a live-in nanny, essential when you have a small baby and a full-time television career, and a growing menagerie. Bailey has two more canine friends – a rottweiler called Mildred and George, an Alsatian, and she also now has two cats, one of whom, inevitably, is called Elvis. Tallulah will have plenty of pets to play with as she grows up.

And her fan base continues to grow. Look her up on the Internet, and there are currently nearly 80,000 searches for Jessie's name alone. There are fan sites devoted to her, with message boards and picture galleries. And her popularity has spread well beyond aficionados of *EastEnders*; she is now a firm favourite with the television viewing public as a whole.

She'll be missed from *EastEnders*, though, that is for sure. It is possible she may one day return to the series, although that is not on the cards at the moment, but what is certain is that she'll be a very hard act to follow. *EastEnders* might have been the making of Jessie, but

Jessie certainly added to the compulsive viewing that is *EastEnders*. As for her trademark catchphrase – 'Oi, what you lookin' at?' – after five years on television, the answer is clear. Jessie… we're looking at you.